This is a technical explanation of the Protocol and the related Memorandum of Understanding signed at Paris on January 13, 2009 (hereinafter the "Protocol" and "Memorandum of Understanding" respectively), amending the Convention between the Government of the United States of America and the Government of the French Republic for the avoidance of double taxation and the prevention of fiscal evasion with respect to taxes on income and capital, signed at Paris on August 31, 1994, as amended by the Protocol signed on December 8, 2004 (together, the "existing Convention").

Negotiations took into account the U.S. Department of the Treasury's current tax treaty policy and the Treasury Department's Model Income Tax Convention, published on November 15, 2006 (the "U.S. Model"). Negotiations also took into account the Model Tax Convention on Income and on Capital, published by the Organisation for Economic Cooperation and Development (the "OECD Model"), and recent tax treaties concluded by both countries.

This Technical Explanation is an official guide to the Protocol and Memorandum of Understanding. It explains policies behind particular provisions, as well as understandings reached during the negotiations with respect to the interpretation and application of the Protocol and Memorandum of Understanding.

References to the "existing Convention" are intended to put various provisions of the Protocol into context. The Technical Explanation does not, however, provide a complete comparison between the provisions of the existing Convention and the amendments made by the Protocol. The Technical Explanation is not intended to provide a complete guide to the existing Convention as amended by the Protocol and Memorandum of Understanding. To the extent that the existing Convention has not been amended by the Protocol and Memorandum of Understanding, the Technical Explanations of the Convention signed at Paris on August 31, 1994 (the "1994 Convention") and the Protocol signed on December 8, 2004 (the "2004 Protocol") remain the official explanation. To the extent that a paragraph from the 1994 Convention or the 2004 Protocol has not been changed, the technical explanations to the 1994 Convention and the 2004 Protocol, respectively, remain the official explanation. References in this Technical Explanation to "he" or "his" should be read to mean "he or she" or "his or her." References to the "Code" are to the Internal Revenue Code of 1986, as amended.

1

On the date of signing of the Protocol, the United States and France also signed a memorandum of understanding relating to the implementation of new paragraphs 5 and 6 of Article 26 (Mutual Agreement Procedure), which provide for binding arbitration of certain disputes between the competent authorities ("Arbitration MOU").

Article I

Article I of the Protocol revises Article 4 (Resident) of the existing Convention by revising paragraph 2 and adding a new paragraph 3. The changes to paragraph 2 clarify the meaning of "resident" in certain cases, and address the treatment of cross-border investments made through certain entities. New paragraph 3 replaces the specific rules in the case of income derived through specified fiscally transparent entities such as partnerships and certain estates and trusts.

The Protocol revises subparagraph b) (iii) of paragraph 2 of Article 4 of the existing Convention and clarifies that a French "société d'investissement à capital variable" (SICAV), "société d'investissement immobilier cotée" (SIIC), and "société de placement à prépondérance immobilière à capital variable" (SPPICAV) will be treated as residents of France for purposes of the Convention. The term "resident of a Contracting State" is defined in paragraph 1 of Article 4 of the Convention. In general, this definition incorporates the definitions of residence in U.S. and French law by referring to a resident as a person who, under the laws of a Contracting State, is liable to tax therein by reason of his domicile, residence, place of management, place of incorporation or any other similar criterion.

New clause (iii) also retains the clarification in the existing Convention that certain entities that are nominally subject to tax but that in practice are rarely required to pay tax also would generally be treated as residents and therefore accorded benefits under the Convention. For example, a U.S. Regulated Investment Company (RIC) and a U.S. Real Estate Investment Trust (REIT) are residents of the United States for purposes of the Convention. Although the income earned by these entities normally is not subject to U.S. tax in the hands of the entity, they are taxable to the extent that they do not currently distribute their profits, and therefore may be regarded as "liable to tax." They also must satisfy a number of requirements under the Code in order to be entitled to special tax treatment.

New subparagraph c) of paragraph 2 of Article 4 clarifies that certain items of income paid from the United States to a French qualified partnership will be considered derived by a resident of France. The provision is intended to ensure that French qualified partnerships are eligible for benefits under Article 4 as amended by the Protocol to the same extent as they were eligible for benefits under subparagraph b) (iv) of paragraph 2 of Article 4 of the existing Convention prior to the entry into force of the Protocol. The provision provides that an item of income paid from the United States to a French qualified partnership is considered derived by a resident of France only to the extent that such income is included currently in the taxable income of a shareholder, associate, or other member that is otherwise treated as a resident of France under the provisions of this

Convention. For purposes of this subparagraph, a French qualified partnership is defined as a partnership that has its place of effective management in France, has not elected to be taxed in France as a corporation, the tax base of which is computed at the partnership level for French tax purposes, and all of the shareholders, associates, or other members of which, pursuant to the tax laws of France, are liable to tax therein in respect of the share of profits of that partnership.

New paragraph 3 addresses special issues presented by fiscally transparent entities. Entities that are fiscally transparent for U.S. tax purposes include partnerships, common investment trusts under section 584, and grantor trusts. This paragraph also applied to U.S. limited liability companies ("LLCs") that are treated as partnerships or as disregarded entities for tax purposes. In general, new paragraph 3 relates to entities that are not subject to tax at the entity level, as distinct from entities that are subject to tax, but with respect to which tax may be relieved under an integrated system.

Because countries may take different views as to when an entity is fiscally transparent, the risk of double taxation and double non-taxation in these cases is relatively high. The intention of new paragraph 3 is to eliminate a number of technical disputes that had arisen under the language of paragraph 2(b)(iv) as it existed prior to the Protocol, and to adopt the modern U.S. tax treaty approach, with certain modifications addressing fiscally transparent entities formed or organized in states with which the source state does not have an agreement containing a provision for the exchange of information with a view to the prevention of tax evasion with the Contracting State from which the income, profit or gains is derived.

New paragraph 3 provides that an item of income, profit or gain derived by a fiscally transparent entity is considered to be derived by a resident of a Contracting State to the extent that the resident is treated under the taxation laws of the State where he is resident as deriving the item of income. This paragraph applies to any resident of a Contracting State who derives income, profit or gain through an entity that is treated as fiscally transparent under the laws of either Contracting State, where such entity is formed or organized in either Contracting State or in a state that has concluded an agreement containing a provision for the exchange of information with a view to the prevention of tax evasion with the Contracting State from which the income, profit, or gain is derived.

For example, if a corporation resident in France distributes a dividend to an entity that is formed or organized in the United States, and is treated as fiscally transparent for U.S. tax purposes, the dividend will be considered derived by a resident of the United States only to the extent that the taxation laws of the United States treat one or more U.S. residents (whose status as U.S. residents is determined, for this purpose, under U.S. tax laws) as deriving the dividend income for U.S. tax purposes. In the case of a partnership, the persons who are, under U.S. tax laws, treated as partners of the entity would normally be the persons whom the U.S. tax laws would treat as deriving the dividend income through the partnership. Thus, it also follows that persons whom the United States treats as partners but who are not U.S. residents for U.S. tax purposes may not claim any benefits under the Convention for the dividend paid to the entity. Although these partners are treated as deriving the income for U.S. tax purposes, they are not residents of the United States for purposes of the Convention. If, however, they are treated as residents of a third country under the provisions of an income tax convention which that country has with France, they may be entitled to claim a benefit under that convention. In contrast, if an entity is organized under U.S. laws and is classified as a corporation for U.S. tax purposes, dividends paid by a corporation resident in France to the U.S. entity will be considered derived by a resident of the United States since the U.S. corporation is treated under U.S. taxation laws as a resident of the United States and as deriving the income.

Because the entity classification rules of the State of residence govern, the results in the examples discussed above would obtain even if the entity were viewed differently under the tax laws of France (e.g., as not fiscally transparent in the first example above where the entity is treated as a partnership for U.S. tax purposes or as fiscally transparent in the second example where the entity is viewed as not fiscally transparent for U.S. tax purposes). Moreover, these results follow regardless of whether the entity is organized in the United States, France, or in a third country, so long as the third country has concluded an agreement containing a provision for the exchange of information with the Contracting State from which the income, profit, or gain is derived. Where income is derived through an entity organized in a third state that has owners resident in one of the Contracting States, the characterization of the entity in that third state is irrelevant for purposes of determining whether the resident is entitled to benefits under the Convention with respect to income derived by the entity. The results follow regardless of whether the entity is disregarded as a separate entity under the laws of one jurisdiction but not the other, such as a single owner entity that is viewed as a branch for U.S. tax purposes and as a corporation for tax purposes under the laws of France.

The following examples illustrate the application of new paragraph 3.

Example 1. Income from sources in France is received by an entity organized under the laws of France, which is treated for U.S. tax purposes as a corporation and is owned by a U.S. shareholder who is a U.S. resident for U.S. tax purposes. Such income is not considered derived by the shareholder of that corporation even if, under the tax laws of France, the entity is treated as fiscally transparent.

Example 2. Income from sources in France is received by XCo, an entity organized in Country X and owned by a U.S. shareholder who is a resident for U.S. tax purposes. XCo is treated for U.S. tax purposes as fiscally transparent. Country X has not concluded an agreement containing a provision for the exchange of information with a view to the prevention of tax evasion with France. Accordingly, the U.S. shareholder is not considered under new paragraph 3 to have derived the French-source income.

These principles also apply to trusts to the extent that they are fiscally transparent in either Contracting State. For example, if X, a resident of France, creates a revocable trust in the United States and names persons resident in a third country as the beneficiaries of the trust, the trust's income would be regarded as being derived by a resident of France only to the extent that the laws of France treat X as deriving the income for its tax purposes, perhaps through application of rules similar to the U.S. "grantor trust" rules.

Paragraph 3 is not an exception to the saving clause of paragraph 4. Accordingly, paragraph 3 does not prevent a Contracting State from taxing an entity that is treated as a resident of that State under its own tax law. For example, if a U.S. LLC with members who are residents of France elects to be taxed as a corporation for U.S. tax purposes, the United States will tax that LLC on its worldwide income on a net basis, without regard to whether France views the LLC as fiscally transparent.

Article II

Article II of the Protocol replaces Article 10 (Dividends) of the existing Convention. Article 10 provides rules for the taxation of dividends paid by a company that is a resident of one Contracting State to a beneficial owner that is a resident of the other Contracting State. The Article provides for full residence country taxation of such dividends and a limited source-State right to tax. Article 10 also provides rules for the imposition of a tax on branch profits by the State of source. Finally, the Article prohibits a State from imposing taxes on a company resident in the other Contracting State, other than a branch profits tax, on undistributed earnings.

Paragraph 1 of Article 10

The right of a shareholder's country of residence to tax dividends arising in the source country is preserved by paragraph 1, which permits a Contracting State to tax its residents on dividends paid to them by a company that is a resident of the other Contracting State. For dividends from any other source paid to a resident, Article 22 (Other Income) grants the residence country exclusive taxing jurisdiction (other than for dividends attributable to a permanent establishment in the other State).

Paragraph 2 of Article 10

The State of source also may tax dividends beneficially owned by a resident of the other State, subject to the limitations of paragraphs 2, 3, and 4. Paragraph 2 generally limits the rate of withholding tax in the State of source on dividends paid by a company resident in that State to 15 percent of the gross amount of the dividend. If, however, the beneficial owner of the dividend is a company resident in France and owns directly shares representing at least 10 percent of the voting stock of the U.S. company paying the dividend, then the U.S. rate of withholding tax is limited to 5 percent of the gross amount of the dividend. Shares are considered voting shares if they provide the power to elect, appoint or replace any person vested with the powers ordinarily exercised by the board of directors of a U.S. corporation.

If the beneficial owner of the dividends is a company resident in the United States that owns, directly or indirectly at least 10 percent of the capital of the French company paying the dividends, then the French rate of withholding tax is limited to 5 percent of the gross amount of the dividend. Subparagraph (a) of paragraph 2 of Article 10 is in all material respects the same as subparagraph (a) of paragraph 2 of Article 10 of the 2004 Convention.

The benefits of paragraph 2 may be granted at the time of payment by means of reduced rate of withholding tax at source. It also is consistent with the paragraph for tax to be withheld at the time of payment at full statutory rates, and the treaty benefit to be granted by means of a subsequent refund so long as such procedures are applied in a reasonable manner.

The determination of whether the ownership threshold for subparagraph 2 is met for purposes of the 5 percent maximum rate of withholding tax is made on the date on which entitlement to the dividend is determined. Thus, in the case of a dividend from a U.S. company, the determination of whether the ownership threshold is met generally would be made on the dividend record date.

The term "beneficial owner" is not defined in the Convention, and is, therefore, defined under the internal law of the State granting treaty benefits (*i.e.*, the source State). The beneficial owner of the dividend for purposes of Article 10 is the person to which the dividend income is attributable for tax purposes under the laws of the source State. Thus, if a dividend paid by a corporation that is a resident of one of the States (as determined under Article 4 (Resident)) is received by a nominee or agent that is a resident of the other State on behalf of a person that is not a resident of that other State, the dividend is not entitled to the benefits of Article 10. However, a dividend received by a nominee on behalf of a resident of that other State would be entitled to benefits. These limitations are confirmed by paragraph 12 of the Commentary to Article 10 of the OECD Model.

Special rules, however, apply to shares that are held through fiscally transparent entities. In that case, the rules of paragraph 3 of Article 4 (Resident) will apply to determine whether the dividends should be treated as having been derived by a resident of a Contracting State. Subject to certain limitations described in paragraph 3 of Article 4, residence State principles shall be used to determine who derives the dividends, to assure that the dividends for which the source State grants benefits of the Convention will be taken into account for tax purposes by a resident of the residence State. Source State principles of beneficial ownership shall then apply to determine whether the person who derives the dividends, or another resident of the other Contracting State, is the beneficial owner of the dividends. The source State may conclude that the person who derives the dividends in the residence State is a mere nominee, agent, conduit, etc., for a third country resident and deny benefits of the Convention. If the person who derives the dividends under paragraph 3 of Article 4 would not be treated under the source State's principles for determining beneficial ownership as a nominee, agent, custodian, conduit, etc., that person will be treated as the beneficial owner of the dividends for purposes of the Convention.

Assume, for instance, that a company resident in France pays a dividend to LLC, an entity which is treated as fiscally transparent for U.S. tax purposes but is treated as a company for French tax purposes. USCo, a company incorporated in the United States, is the sole interest holder in LLC. Paragraph 3 of Article 4 provides that USCo derives the dividend. France's principles of beneficial ownership shall then be applied to USCo. If under the laws of France USCo is found not to be the beneficial owner of the dividend, USCo will not be entitled to the benefits of Article 10 with respect to such dividend. The payment may be entitled to benefits, however, if USCo is found to be a nominee, agent, custodian or conduit for another person who is a resident of the United States.

If in the above example LLC were formed or organized in a country that has not concluded an agreement containing a provision for the exchange of information with a view to the prevention of tax evasion with France, the dividend will not be treated as derived by a resident of the United States for purposes of the Convention. However, LLC may still be entitled to the benefits of the French tax treaty, if any, with its country of residence.

Beyond identifying the person to whom the principles of beneficial ownership shall be applied, the principles of paragraph 3 of Article 4 will also apply when determining whether other requirements, such as whether the ownership threshold of subparagraph 2(a) of Article 10 has been satisfied.

For example, assume that FranceCo, a company that is a resident of France, owns all of the outstanding shares in ThirdDE, an entity that is disregarded for U.S. tax purposes that is resident in a third country. ThirdDE owns 100 percent of the stock of USCo. France views ThirdDE as fiscally transparent under its domestic law, and taxes FranceCo currently on the income derived by ThirdDE. ThirdDE is formed or organized in a country that has concluded an agreement containing a provision for the exchange of information with a view to the prevention of tax evasion with the United States. In this case, FranceCo is treated as deriving the dividends paid by USCo under paragraph 3 of Article 4. Moreover, FranceCo is treated as owning the shares of USCo directly. The Convention does not address what constitutes direct ownership for purposes of Article 10. As a result, whether ownership is direct is determined under the internal law of the State granting treaty benefits (*i.e.*, the source State) unless the context otherwise requires. Accordingly, a company that holds stock through such an entity will generally be considered to own directly such stock for purposes of Article 10.

This result may change, however, if ThirdDE is regarded as non-fiscally transparent under the laws of France, or if ThirdDE is formed or organized in a country that has not concluded an agreement containing a provision for the exchange of information with a view to the prevention of tax evasion with the United States. If either of these conditions applies, the income will not be treated as derived by a resident of France for purposes of the Convention. However, ThirdDE may still be entitled to the benefits of the U.S. tax treaty, if any, with its country of residence.

7

The same principles would apply in determining whether companies holding shares through fiscally transparent entities such as partnerships, trusts, and estates would qualify for benefits. As a result, companies holding shares through such entities may be able to claim the benefits of subparagraph (a) of paragraph 2 of Article 10 under certain circumstances. The lower rate applies when the company's proportionate share of the shares held by the intermediate entity meets the 10 percent threshold, and the company meets the requirements of Article 4(3). Whether this ownership threshold is satisfied may be difficult to determine and often will require an analysis of the partnership or trust agreement.

Paragraph 3 of Article 10

Paragraph 3 provides exclusive residence-country taxation (*i.e.,* an elimination of withholding tax) with respect to certain dividends distributed by a company that is a resident of one Contracting State to a resident of the other Contracting State. As described further below, this elimination of withholding tax is available with respect to certain inter-company dividends and with respect to certain pension funds.

Subparagraph (a) of paragraph 3 provides for the elimination of withholding tax on dividends beneficially owned by a company that has owned, directly or indirectly through one or more residents of either Contracting State, 80 percent or more of the voting power of the company paying the dividend for the 12-month period ending on the date entitlement to the dividend is determined. The determination of whether the beneficial owner of the dividends owns at least 80 percent of the voting power of the company is made by taking into account stock owned both directly and indirectly through one or more residents of either Contracting State.

Eligibility for the elimination of withholding tax provided by subparagraph (a) is subject to additional restrictions based on, and supplementing, the rules of Article 30 (Limitation on Benefits of the Convention). Accordingly, a company that meets the holding requirements described above will qualify for the benefits of paragraph 3 only if it also: (1) meets the "publicly traded" test of subparagraph 2(c) of Article 30, (2) meets the "ownership-base erosion" and "active trade or business" tests described in subparagraph 2(e) and paragraph 4 of Article 30, (3) meets the "derivative benefits" test of paragraph 3 of Article 30, or (4) is granted the benefits of paragraph 3 of Article 10 by the competent authority of the source State pursuant to paragraph 6 of Article 30.

These restrictions are necessary because of the increased pressure on the limitation on benefits tests resulting from the fact that the United States has relatively few treaties that provide for such elimination of withholding tax on inter-company dividends. The additional restrictions are intended to prevent companies from re-organizing in order to become eligible for the elimination of withholding tax in circumstances where the limitation on benefits provision does not provide sufficient protection against treaty shopping.

For example, assume that ThirdCo is a company resident in a third country that does not have a tax treaty with the United States providing for the elimination of withholding tax on inter-company dividends. ThirdCo owns directly 100 percent of the issued and outstanding voting stock of USCo, a U.S. company, and of FCo, a French company. FCo is a substantial company that manufactures widgets; USCo distributes those widgets in the United States. If ThirdCo contributes to FCo all the stock of USCo, dividends paid by USCo to FCo would qualify for treaty benefits under the active trade or business test of paragraph 4 of Article 30. However, allowing ThirdCo to qualify for the elimination of withholding tax, which is not available to it under the third state's treaty with the United States (if any), would encourage treaty shopping.

In order to prevent this type of treaty shopping, paragraph 3 requires FCo to meet the ownership-base erosion requirements of subparagraph 2(e) of Article 30 in addition to the active trade or business test of paragraph 4 of Article 30. Because FCo is wholly owned by a third country resident, FCo could not qualify for the elimination of withholding tax on dividends from USCo under the combined ownership-base erosion and active trade or business tests of paragraph 3(b). Consequently, FCo would need to qualify under another test in paragraph 3 or obtain discretionary relief from the competent authority under Article 30(6). For purpose of Article 10(3)(b), it is not sufficient for a company to qualify for treaty benefits generally under the active trade or business test or the ownership-base erosion test unless it qualifies for treaty benefits under both.

Alternatively, companies that are publicly traded or subsidiaries of publicly-traded companies will generally qualify for the elimination of withholding tax. Thus, a company that is a resident of France and that meets the requirements of Article 30(2)(c)(i) or (ii) will be entitled to the elimination of withholding tax, subject to the 12-month holding period requirement of Article 10(3).

In addition, under Article 10(3)(c), a company that is a resident of a Contracting State may also qualify for the elimination of withholding tax on dividends if it satisfies the derivative benefits test of paragraph 3 of Article 30. Thus, a French company that owns all of the stock of a U.S. corporation may qualify for the elimination of withholding tax if it is wholly-owned by a company that falls within the definition of "equivalent beneficiary" in Article 30(7)(f).

The derivative benefits test may also provide benefits to U.S. companies receiving dividends from French subsidiaries because of the effect of the Parent-Subsidiary Directive in the European Union. Under that directive, inter-company dividends paid within the European Union are free of withholding tax. Under subparagraph (g) of paragraph 7 of Article 30 that directive will be taken into account in determining whether the owner of a U.S. company receiving dividends from a French company is an equivalent beneficiary. Thus, a company that is a resident of a member state of the European Union will, by virtue of the Parent-Subsidiary Directive, satisfy the requirements of Article 30(7)(f)(1)(bb) with respect to any dividends received by its U.S. subsidiary from a French company. For example, assume USCo is a wholly-owned subsidiary of ICo, an Italian publicly-traded company. USCo owns all of the shares of FCo, a French company. If FCo were to pay dividends directly to ICo, those dividends would be exempt from withholding tax in France by reason of the Parent-Subsidiary Directive. If ICo meets the other conditions to be an equivalent beneficiary under subparagraph 7(f) of Article 30, it will be treated as an equivalent beneficiary by reason of subparagraph 7(g) of that article.

A company also may qualify for the elimination of withholding tax pursuant to Article 10(3)(c) if it is owned by seven or fewer U.S. or French residents who qualify as an "equivalent beneficiary" and meet the other requirements of the derivative benefits provision. This rule may apply, for example, to certain French corporate joint venture vehicles that are closely-held by a few French resident individuals.

Subparagraph (f) of paragraph 7 of Article 30 contains a specific rule of application intended to ensure that for purposes of applying Article 10(3) certain joint ventures, not just wholly-owned subsidiaries, can qualify for benefits. For example, assume that the United States were to enter into a treaty with Country X, a member of the European Union, that includes a provision identical to Article 10(3). USCo is 100 percent owned by FCo, a French company, which in turn is owned 49 percent by PCo, a French publicly-traded company, and 51 percent by XCo, a publicly-traded company that is resident in Country X. In the absence of a special rule for interpreting the derivative benefits provision, each of PCo and XCo would be treated as owning only their proportionate share of the shares held by FCo in USCo. If that rule were applied in this situation, neither PCo nor XCo would be an equivalent beneficiary, because neither would meet the 80 percent ownership test with respect to USCo. However, since both PCo and XCo are residents of countries that have treaties with the United States that provide for elimination of withholding tax on inter-company dividends, it is appropriate to provide benefits to FCo in this case.

Accordingly, the definition of "equivalent beneficiary" includes a rule of application that is intended to ensure that such joint ventures qualify for the benefits of Article 10(3). Under that rule, each of the shareholders is treated as owning shares of USCo with the same percentage of voting power as the shares held by FCo for purposes of determining whether it would be entitled to an equivalent rate of withholding tax. This rule is necessary because of the high ownership threshold for qualification for the elimination of withholding tax on inter-company dividends.

If a company does not qualify for the elimination of withholding tax under any of the foregoing objective tests, it may request a determination from the relevant competent authority pursuant to paragraph 6 of Article 30. Benefits will be granted with respect to an item of income if the competent authority of the Contracting State in which the income arises determines that the establishment, acquisition or maintenance of such resident and the conduct of its operations did not have as one of its principal purposes the obtaining of benefits under the Convention.

Paragraph 4 of Article 10

Paragraph 4 provides that paragraphs 2 and 3 do not affect the taxation of the profits out of which the dividends are paid. The taxation by a Contracting State of the income of its resident companies is governed by the internal law of the Contracting State, subject to the provisions of paragraph 3 of Article 25 (Non-Discrimination).

Paragraph 5 of Article 10

Paragraph 5 imposes limitations on the rate reductions provided by paragraphs 2 and 3 in the case of dividends paid by a RIC, a REIT, a SICAV, a SIIC, or a SPPICAV.

Subparagraph 5(a) provides that dividends paid by a RIC, a REIT, a SICAV, a SIIC, or a SPPICAV are not eligible for the 5 percent rate of withholding tax provided in subparagraph 2(a) or the elimination of withholding tax provided in paragraph 3.

The first sentence of subparagraph 5(b) provides that the 15 percent maximum rate of withholding tax of subparagraph 2(b) applies to dividends paid by RICs or SICAVs.

The second sentence of subparagraph 5(b) provides that the 15 percent rate of withholding tax also applies to dividends paid by a REIT, a SIIC, or a SPPICAV, provided that one of the three following conditions is met. First, the beneficial owner of the dividends is an individual or a pension trust or other organization maintained exclusively to administer or provide retirement or employee benefits that is established or sponsored by a resident, in either case holding an interest of not more than 10 percent in the REIT, SIIC, or SPPICAV. Second, the dividends are paid with respect to a class of stock that is publicly traded and the beneficial owner of the dividend is a person holding an interest of not more than 5 percent of any class of the REIT, SIIC, or SPPICAV's shares. Third, the beneficial owner of the dividends holds an interest in the REIT, SIIC, or SPPICAV of not more than 10 percent and, in the case of a REIT, the REIT is "diversified."

Subparagraph 5(c) provides that a REIT is diversified if the gross value of no single interest in real property held by the REIT exceeds 10 percent of the gross value of the REIT's total interest in real property. Foreclosure property is not considered an interest in real property, and a REIT holding a partnership interest is treated as owning directly its proportionate share of any interest in real property held by the partnership.

The restrictions set out above are intended to prevent the use of RICs or REITs to gain inappropriate U.S. tax benefits, or the use of SICAVs, SIICs, or SPPICAVs to gain inappropriate French tax benefits. For example, a company resident in France that wishes to hold a diversified portfolio of U.S. corporate shares could hold the portfolio directly and would bear a U.S. withholding tax of 15 percent on all of the dividends that it receives. Alternatively, it could hold the same diversified portfolio by purchasing 10 percent or more of the interests in a RIC that in turn held the portfolio. Absent the

11

special rule in paragraph 5, such use of the RIC could transform portfolio dividends, taxable in the United States under the Convention at a 15 percent maximum rate of withholding tax, into direct investment dividends taxable at a 5 percent maximum rate of withholding tax or eligible for the elimination of source-country withholding tax on dividends provided in paragraph 3.

Similarly, a resident of France directly holding U.S. real property would pay U.S. tax upon the sale of the property either at a 30 percent rate of withholding tax on the gross income or at graduated rates on the net income. As in the preceding example, by placing the real property in a REIT, the investor could, absent a special rule, transform income from the sale of real estate into dividend income from the REIT, taxable at the rates provided in Article 10, significantly reducing the U.S. tax that otherwise would be imposed. Paragraph 5 prevents this result and thereby avoids a disparity between the taxation of direct real estate investments and real estate investments made through REITs. In the cases in which paragraph 5 allows a dividend from a REIT to be eligible for the 15 percent rate of withholding tax, the holding in the REIT is not considered the equivalent of a direct holding in the underlying real property.

Paragraph 6 of Article 10

Paragraph 6 is in all material respects the same as paragraph 5 of Article 10 of the existing Convention. Paragraph 6 defines the term dividends broadly and flexibly. The definition is intended to cover all arrangements that yield a return on an equity investment in a corporation as determined under the tax law of the State of source, as well as arrangements that might be developed in the future.

The term includes income from shares, "jouissance" shares or rights, mining shares, founders' shares, or other rights (not being debt claims), participating in profits, as well as income derived from other rights that is subjected to the same taxation treatment as income from shares by the laws of the Contracting State of which the company making the distribution is a resident. Thus, a constructive dividend that results from a non-arm's length transaction between a corporation and a related party is a dividend. In the case of the United States the term dividend includes amounts treated as a dividend under U.S. law upon the sale or redemption of shares or upon a transfer of shares in a reorganization. See, e.g., Rev. Rul. 92-85, 1992-2 C.B. 69 (sale of foreign subsidiary's stock to U.S. sister company is a deemed dividend to extent of the subsidiary's and siter company's earnings and profits). Further, a distribution from a U.S. publicly traded limited partnership, which is taxed as a corporation under U.S. law, is a dividend for purposes of Article 10. However, a distribution by a limited liability company is not taxable by the United States under Article 10, provided the limited liability company is not characterized as an association taxable as a corporation under U.S. law.

The term "dividends" also includes income from arrangements, including debt obligations, that carry the right to participate in profits or that are determined with reference to profits of the issuer or one of its associated enterprises, to the extent that such income is characterized as a dividend under the law of the source State. A payment

12

denominated as interest that is made by a thinly capitalized corporation may be treated as a dividend to the extent that the debt is recharacterized as equity under the laws of the source State. Distributions to directors as compensation for their services are not treated as dividends under this Article, but as directors' fees under Article 16 (Directors' Fees). As such they are taxable in France to the extent that the services are performed in France. The provisions of this Article also apply to beneficial owners of dividends that hold depository receipts in place of the shares themselves.

Paragraph 7 of Article 10

Paragraph 7 is in all material respects the same as paragraph 6 of the Article 10 of the existing Convention. Paragraph 7 excludes from the general source State limitations under paragraphs 2 through 4 dividends attributable to a permanent establishment or fixed base of the beneficial owner in the source State. In such case, the rules of Article 7 (Business Profits) or 14 (Independent Personal Services) shall apply. Accordingly, the dividends will be taxed on a net basis using the rates and rules of taxation generally applicable to residents of the State in which the permanent establishment or fixed base is located, as such rules may be modified by the Convention.

Paragraph 8 of Article 10

Paragraph 8 is substantially similar to paragraph 7 of Article 10 of the existing Convention. Paragraph 8 permits a Contracting State to impose a branch profits tax on a company resident in the other Contracting State. The tax is in addition to other taxes permitted by the Convention.

Paragraph 8 clarifies that such tax may be imposed (subject to the limitations described in paragraph 9 of Article 10) only on the portion of the business profits of the company attributable to the permanent establishment and the portion of the income of the company derived from real property in the Contracting State imposing the branch profits tax that is taxed on a net basis under Article 6 (Income from Real Property), or that is realized as gains taxable in that State under paragraph 1 of Article 13 (Capital Gains). In the case of the United States, the imposition of such tax is limited to the portion of the aforementioned items of income and profits that represents the "dividend equivalent amount." In the case of France, the imposition of such tax is limited to the portion of the aforementioned items of income and profits that is included in the base of the French withholding tax in accordance with the provisions of Article 115 "quinquies" of the French tax code.

Consistency principles prohibit a taxpayer from applying provisions of the Code and this Convention inconsistently. In the context of the branch profits tax, this consistency requirement means that if a French company uses the principles of Article 7 to determine its U.S. taxable income then it must also use those principles to determine its dividend equivalent amount. Similarly, if the French company instead uses the Code to determine its U.S. taxable income it must also use the Code to determine its dividend equivalent amount. As in the case of Article 7, if a French company, for example, does not from year to year consistently apply the Code or the Convention to determine its dividend equivalent amount, then the French company must make appropriate adjustments or recapture amounts that would otherwise be subject to U.S. branch profits tax if it had consistently applied the Code or the Convention to determine its dividend equivalent amount from year to year.

Paragraph 9 of Article 10

Paragraph 9 limits the rate of the branch profits tax that may be imposed under paragraph 8 to 5 percent. Paragraph 9 also provides that the branch profits tax shall not be imposed on a company in any case if certain requirements are met. In general, these requirements provide rules for a branch that parallel the rules for when a dividend paid by a subsidiary will be subject to exclusive residence-country taxation (*i.e.*, the elimination of source-country withholding tax). Accordingly, the branch profits tax cannot be imposed in the case of a company that: (1) meets the "publicly traded" test of subparagraph 2(c) of Article 30, (2) meets the "ownership-base erosion" and "active trade or business" tests described in subparagraph 2(e) and paragraph 4 of Article 30, (3) meets the "derivative benefits" test of paragraph 3 of Article 30, or (4) is granted benefits with respect to the elimination of the branch profits tax by the competent authority pursuant to paragraph 6 of Article 30. If the company did not meet any of those tests, but otherwise qualified for benefits under Article 30, then the branch profits tax would apply at a rate of 5 percent, unless the company is granted benefits with respect to the elimination of the branch profits tax by the competent authority pursuant to paragraph 6 of Article 30.

It is intended that paragraph 9 apply equally if a taxpayer determines its taxable income under the laws of a Contracting State or under the provisions of Article 7. For example, as discussed above in the explanation to paragraph 8, consistency principles require a French company that determines its U.S. taxable income under the Code to also determine its dividend equivalent amount under the Code. In that case, paragraph 9 would apply even though the French company did not determine its dividend equivalent amount using the principles of Article 7.

Paragraph 10 of Article 10

Paragraph 10 is in all material respects the same as paragraph 8 of Article 10 of the existing Convention. The right of a Contracting State to tax dividends paid by a company that is a resident of the other Contracting State is restricted by paragraph 10 to cases in which the dividends are paid to a resident of that Contracting State or are attributable to a permanent establishment or fixed base in that Contracting State. In the former case, the country of residence may tax the dividends by virtue of paragraph 2 of Article 29 (Miscellaneous Provisions). In the latter case, the dividends are taxable by France or the United States under Article 7 (Business Profits) or 14 (Independent Personal Services). Thus, a Contracting State may not impose a "secondary" withholding tax on dividends paid by a nonresident company out of earnings and profits from that Contracting State.

The paragraph also restricts the right of a Contracting State to impose corporate level taxes on undistributed profits, other than a branch profits tax. The paragraph does not restrict a State's right to tax its resident shareholders on undistributed earnings of a corporation resident in the other State. Thus, the authority of the United States to impose taxes on subpart F income and on earnings deemed invested in U.S. property, and its tax on income of a passive foreign investment company that is a qualified electing fund is in no way restricted by this provision.

Relationship to Other Articles

Notwithstanding the foregoing limitations on source country taxation of dividends, the saving clause of paragraph 2 of Article 29 (Miscellaneous Provisions), as amended by the Protocol, permits the United States to tax dividends received by its residents and citizens, subject to the special foreign tax credit rules of paragraph 2(b) of Article 24 (Relief from Double Taxation), as renumbered by paragraph 1 of Article VIII of the Protocol, as if the Convention had not come into effect.

The benefits of Article 10 are also subject to the provisions of Article 30. Thus, if a resident of a Contracting State is the beneficial owner of dividends paid by a corporation that is a resident of the other Contracting State, the shareholder must qualify for treaty benefits under at least one of the tests of Article 30 in order to receive the benefits of Article 10.

Article III

Article III of the Protocol revises Article 12 (Royalties) of the Convention by generally granting to the State of residence the exclusive right to tax royalties beneficially owned by its residents and arising in the other Contracting State. Prior to its amendment by the Protocol, the existing Convention permitted the source State to tax royalties beneficially owned by a resident of the other Contracting State at a maximum withholding rate of 5 percent of the gross amount of the royalty. To reflect the elimination of source-country taxation of royalties, Article III of the Protocol replaces paragraph 1, deletes paragraphs 2 and 3, and revises paragraphs 4 and 5 of Article 12 of the existing Convention.

Paragraph 1

Paragraph 1 of Article III of the Protocol replaces paragraph 1 of Article 12 of the Convention. New paragraph 1 generally grants to the State of residence the exclusive right to tax royalties beneficially owned by its residents and arising in the other Contracting State.

The term "beneficial owner" is not defined in the Convention, and is, therefore, defined under the internal law of the State granting treaty benefits (*i.e.*, the State of source). The beneficial owner of the royalty for purposes of Article 12 is the person to which the income is attributable under the laws of the source State. Thus, if a royalty arising in a Contracting State is received by a nominee or agent that is a resident of the other State on behalf of a person that is not a resident of that other State, the royalty is not entitled to the benefits of Article 12. However, a royalty received by a nominee on behalf of a resident of that other State would be entitled to benefits. These limitations are confirmed by paragraph 4 of the OECD Commentary to Article 12.

Paragraph 2

Paragraph 2 deletes paragraphs 2 through 5 of Article 12 of the existing Convention.

Paragraph 3

Paragraph 3 amends Article 12 of the existing Convention by adding new paragraphs 2 and 3. New paragraph 2 defines the term "royalties" as used in Article 12 to mean any consideration for the use of, or the right to use, any copyright of literary, artistic, or scientific work or any neighboring right (including reproduction rights and performing rights), any cinematographic film, sound or picture recording, any software, any patent, trademark, design or model, plan, secret formula or process, or other like right or property, or for information concerning industrial, commercial, or scientific experience. The term "royalties" also includes gains derived from the alienation of any right or property described in the previous sentence that are contingent on the productivity, use, or further alienation thereof. The term "royalties" does not include income from leasing personal property.

The term "royalties" is defined in the Convention and therefore is generally independent of domestic law. Certain terms used in the definition are not defined in the Convention, but these may be defined under domestic tax law. For example, the term "secret process or formulas" is found in the Code, and its meaning has been elaborated in the context of sections 351 and 367. See Rev. Rul. 55-17, 1955-1 C.B. 388; Rev. Rul. 64-56, 1964-1 C.B. 133; Rev. Proc. 69-19, 1969-2 C.B. 301.

Consideration for the use or right to use cinematographic films, or works on film, tape, or other means of reproduction of audio or video is specifically included in the definition of royalties. It is intended that, with respect to any subsequent technological advances in the field of audio or video recording, consideration received for the use of audio or video recording using such technology will also be included in the definition of royalties.

If an artist who is resident in one Contracting State records a performance in the other Contracting State, retains a copyrighted interest in a recording, and receives payments for the right to use the recording based on the sale or public playing of the recording, then the right of such other Contracting State to tax those payments is governed by Article 12. See Boulez v. Commissioner, 83 T.C. 584 (1984), aff'd, 810 F.2d 209 (D.C. Cir. 1986). By contrast, if the artist earns in the other Contracting State income covered by Article 17 (Artistes and Sportsmen), for example, endorsement income from the artist's attendance at a film screening, and if such income also is attributable to one of the rights described in Article 12 (*e.g.*, the use of the artist's photograph in promoting the screening), Article 17 and not Article 12 is applicable to such income.

The term "industrial, commercial, or scientific experience" (sometimes referred to as "know-how") has the meaning ascribed to it in paragraph 11 *et seq.* of the Commentary to Article 12 of the OECD Model. Consistent with that meaning, the term may include information that is ancillary to a right otherwise giving rise to royalties, such as a patent or secret process.

Know-how also may include, in limited cases, technical information that is conveyed through technical or consultancy services. It does not include general educational training of the user's employees, nor does it include information developed especially for the user, such as a technical plan or design developed according to the user's specifications. Thus, as provided in paragraph 11.3 of the Commentary to Article 12 of the OECD Model, the term "royalties" does not include payments received as consideration for after-sales service, for services rendered by a seller to a purchaser under a warranty, or for pure technical assistance.

The term "royalties" also does not include payments for professional services (such as architectural, engineering, legal, managerial, medical, software development services). For example, income from the design of a refinery by an engineer (even if the engineer employed know-how in the process of rendering the design) or the production of a legal brief by a lawyer is not income from the transfer of know-how taxable under Article 12, but is income from services taxable under either Article 7 (Business Profits) or Article 14 (Independent Personal Services). Professional services may be embodied in property that gives rise to royalties, however. Thus, if a professional contracts to develop patentable property and retains rights in the resulting property under the development contract, subsequent license payments made for those rights would be royalties.

New paragraph 3 of Article 12 is in all material respects the same as paragraph 5 of Article 12 of the existing Convention. This paragraph provides an exception to the rule of new paragraph 1 that gives the State of residence exclusive taxing jurisdiction in cases where the beneficial owner of the royalties carries on business through a permanent establishment or fixed base in the State of source and the royalties are attributable to that permanent establishment or fixed base. In such cases, the provisions of Article 7 (Business Profits) or Article 14 (Independent Personal Services), as the case may be, will apply. The source State may not impose tax on copyright royalties described in new subparagraph 2a) that are beneficially owned by a resident of the other Contracting State.

Paragraph 4

Paragraph 4 of Article III of the Protocol renumbers paragraphs 6 and 7 of Article 12 of the Convention prior to amendment by the Protocol as paragraphs 4 and 5, respectively. New paragraphs 4 and 5 are identical to paragraphs 6 and 7 of Article 12 of the existing Convention, respectively.

Relationship to Other Articles

Notwithstanding the foregoing limitations on source country taxation of royalties, the saving clause of paragraph 2 of Article 29 (Miscellaneous Provisions), as amended by the Protocol, permits the United States to tax its residents and citizens, subject to the special foreign tax credit rules of paragraph 2(b) of Article 24 (Relief from Double Taxation), as renumbered by paragraph 1 of Article VIII of the Protocol, as if the Convention had not come into force.

As with other benefits of the Convention, the benefits of Article 12 are available to a resident of a Contracting State only if such resident qualifies for treaty benefits under Article 30 (Limitation on Benefits of the Convention).

Article IV

Article IV of the Protocol replaces paragraph 5 of Article 13 (Capital Gains) of the existing Convention. Paragraph 5 is in all material respects the same as paragraph 5 of Article 13 of the existing Convention. The only difference is that a reference to paragraph 2 of Article 12 (Royalties) has been revised to conform with the changes made to Article 12 by Article III of the Protocol.

Article V

Article V of the Protocol revises paragraph 1 of Article 17 (Artistes and Sportsmen) of the existing Convention. Paragraph 1 is in all material respects the same as paragraph 1 of Article 17 of the existing Convention. The only difference is that the reference to "French francs" has been replaced with a reference to "euros."

Article VI

Article VI of the Protocol revises paragraph 1 of Article 18 (Pensions) of the Convention. Paragraph 1 of Article 18 of the existing Convention provides for exclusive source country taxation of social security benefits, distributions from pensions and other similar remuneration arising in one Contracting State in consideration of past employment paid to a resident of the other Contracting State. The Protocol revision clarifies that, notwithstanding the saving clause of paragraph 2 of Article 29 (Miscellaneous Provisions) of the Convention, and pursuant to the provisions of paragraph 3 of Article 29, France has the exclusive jurisdiction to tax payments under its social security or similar legislation to a resident of France who is a citizen of the United States.

Article VII

Article VII of the Protocol replaces Article 22 (Other Income) of the existing Convention. Revised Article 22 conforms with the corresponding U.S. Model provision. The Article generally assigns taxing jurisdiction over income not dealt with in the other Articles of the Convention to the State of residence of the beneficial owner of the income. In order for an item of income to be "dealt with" in another article it must be the type of income described in the Article and, in most cases, it must have its source in a Contracting State. For example, all royalty income that arises in a Contracting State and that is beneficially owned by a resident of the other Contracting State is "dealt with" in Article 12 (Royalties). However, profits derived in the conduct of a business are "dealt with" in Article 7 (Business Profits) whether or not they have their source in one of the Contracting States.

Examples of items of income covered by Article 22 include income from gambling, punitive (but not compensatory) damages and covenants not to compete. The Article would also apply to income from a variety of financial transactions, where such income does not arise in the course of the conduct of a trade or business. For example, income from notional principal contracts and other derivatives would fall within Article 22 if derived by persons not engaged in the trade or business of dealing in such instruments, unless such instruments were being used to hedge risks arising in a trade or business. It would also apply to securities lending fees derived by an institutional investor. Further, in most cases guarantee fees paid within an intercompany group would be covered by Article 22, unless the guarantor were engaged in the business of providing such guarantees to unrelated parties.

Article 22 also applies to items of income that are not dealt with in the other articles because of their source or some other characteristic. For example, Article 11 (Interest) addresses only the taxation of interest arising in a Contracting State. Interest arising in a third State that is not attributable to a permanent establishment, therefore, is subject to Article 22.

Distributions from partnerships are not generally dealt with under Article 22 because partnership distributions generally do not constitute income. Under the Code, partners include in income their distributive share of partnership income annually, and partnership distributions themselves generally do not give rise to income. This would also be the case under U.S. law with respect to distributions from trusts. Trust income and distributions that, under the Code, have the character of the associated distributable net income would generally be covered by another article of the Convention. See Code section 641 et seq.

Paragraph 1 of Article 22

The general rule of Article 22 is contained in paragraph 1. Items of income not dealt with in other articles and beneficially owned by a resident of a Contracting State will be taxable only in the State of residence. This exclusive right of taxation applies whether or not the residence State exercises its right to tax the income covered by the Article.

The reference in this paragraph to "items of income beneficially owned by a resident of a Contracting State" rather than simply "items of income of a resident of a Contracting State," as in the OECD Model, is intended merely to make explicit the implicit understanding in other treaties that the exclusive residence taxation provided by paragraph 1 applies only when a resident of a Contracting State is the beneficial owner of the income. Thus, source taxation of income not dealt with in other articles of the Convention is not limited by paragraph 1 if it is nominally paid to a resident of the other Contracting State, but is beneficially owned by a resident of a third State. However, income received by a nominee on behalf of a resident of that other State would be entitled to benefits.

The term "beneficially owned" is not defined in the Convention, and is, therefore, defined as under the internal law of the State granting treaty benefits (*i.e.*, the source State). The person who beneficially owns the income for purposes of Article 22 is the person to which the income is attributable for tax purposes under the laws of the source State.

Paragraph 2 of Article 22

This paragraph provides an exception to the general rule of paragraph 1 for income that is attributable to a permanent establishment or a fixed base maintained in a Contracting State by a resident of the other Contracting State. The taxation of such income is governed by the provisions of Article 7 (Business Profits) or Article 14 (Independent Personal Services), as the case may be. Therefore, income arising outside the United States that is attributable to a permanent establishment or a fixed base maintained in the United States by a resident of the other Contracting State generally would be taxable by the United States under the provisions of Article 7 or Article 14. This would be true even if the income is sourced in a third State.

Relationship to Other Articles

This Article is subject to the saving clause of paragraph 2 of Article 29 (Miscellaneous Provisions). Thus, the United States may tax the income of a resident of the other Contracting State that is not dealt with elsewhere in the Convention, if that resident is a citizen of the United States. The Article is also subject to the provisions of Article 30 (Limitation on Benefits). Thus, if a resident of the other Contracting State earns income that falls within the scope of paragraph 1, but that is taxable by the United States under U.S. law, the income would be exempt from U.S. tax under the provisions of this Article only if the resident satisfies one of the tests of Article 30 for entitlement to benefits.

Article VIII

Paragraph 1

Paragraph 1 revises the numbering incorporated in the alternat of the United States of the existing Convention. In both the English and French versions of the United States alternat, what is paragraph 1 of Article 24 (Relief From Double Taxation) of the existing Convention is renumbered paragraph 2, and what is paragraph 2 of Article 24 (Relief From Double Taxation) of the existing Convention is renumbered paragraph 1. This change is intended to make the numbering of the paragraphs of Article 24 of the Convention in the alternat of the United States and the alternat of France consistent.

Paragraph 2

Paragraph 2 revises what was subparagraph 2(a)(iii) of the United States alternat of the existing Convention, and is renumbered subparagraph 1(a)(iii) by paragraph 1 of this Article of the Protocol. The revision deletes the reference to Article 12 (Royalties) in subparagraph 1(a)(iii). This revision is consistent with the Protocol's revision of paragraph 1 of Article 12, to provide for exclusive residence State taxation of royalties beneficially owned by its residents and arising in the other Contracting State. Royalties are covered under subparagraph 1(a) as revised by the Protocol, but are addressed under clause (i), as income other than that referred to in clauses (ii) and (iii).

Paragraph 3

Paragraph 3 revises clause (i) of subparagraph b) of paragraph 1 of Article 24, as renumbered by paragraph 1 of this Article of the Protocol. The Protocol updates cross-references and makes them consistent with amendments made by this Protocol to other articles of the Convention.

Paragraph 4

Paragraph 4 revises clause (i) of subparagraph e) of paragraph 1 of Article 24, as renumbered by paragraph 1 of this Article of the Protocol, to clarify that France may continue to allow companies resident in France to elect to be taxed on a worldwide basis and allow a tax credit, instead of applying its general system of exempting foreign business income.

Paragraph 5

Paragraph 5 deletes subparagraph (c) of paragraph 2 of Article 24 of the Convention, as amended by paragraph 1 of this Article of the Protocol. The provision was previously intended to ensure that French government employees performing government services in the United States who were dual nationals (*i.e.*, U.S. citizens as well as nationals of France) would not be subject to double taxation. Under new paragraph 9 of Article 29 (Miscellaneous Provisions) of the Convention, as added by the

Protocol, remuneration for such services by such persons is taxable only in the United States, and therefore subparagraph (c) of paragraph 2 of Article 24 of the Convention (as it is numbered subsequent to the amendment provided for in paragraph 1 of this Article) is not necessary.

Article IX

Paragraphs 1 and 2 revise paragraphs 2 and 3 of Article 25 (Non-Discrimination), respectively. The Protocol updates cross-references and makes them consistent with amendments made by this Protocol to other articles of the Convention.

Article X

Article X of the Protocol replaces paragraph 5 of Article 26 (Mutual Agreement Procedure) of the Convention with new paragraphs 5 and 6. New paragraphs 5 and 6 provide a mandatory binding arbitration proceeding (Arbitration Proceeding). The Arbitration MOU provides additional rules and procedures that apply to a case considered under the arbitration provisions.

New paragraph 5 provides that a case shall be resolved through arbitration when the competent authorities have endeavored but are unable to reach a complete agreement regarding a case and the following three conditions are satisfied. First, tax returns have been filed with at least one of the Contracting States with respect to the taxable years at issue in the case. Second, the case is not a case that the competent authorities agree before the date on which arbitration proceedings would otherwise have begun, is not suitable for determination by arbitration. Third, all concerned persons and their authorized representatives agree, according to the provisions of subparagraph (d) of paragraph 6, not to disclose to any other person any information received during the course of the arbitration proceeding from either Contracting State or the arbitration board, other than the determination of the board (confidentiality agreement). The confidentiality agreement may also be executed by any concerned person that has the legal authority to bind any other concerned person on the matter. For example, a parent corporation with the legal authority to bind its subsidiary with respect to confidentiality may execute a comprehensive confidentiality agreement on its own behalf and that of its subsidiary.

New paragraph 5 provides that an unresolved case shall not be submitted to arbitration if a decision on such case has already been rendered by a court or administrative tribunal of either Contracting State.

The United States and France have agreed in the Arbitration MOU that binding arbitration will be used to determine the application of the Convention in respect of any case where the competent authorities have endeavored but are unable to reach an agreement under Article 26 regarding such application. The competent authorities may, however, agree that the particular case is not suitable for determination by arbitration.

New paragraph 6 provides additional rules and definitions to be used in applying the arbitration provisions.

Subparagraph 6(a) provides that the term "concerned person" means the person that brought the case to competent authority for consideration under Article 26 and includes all other persons, if any, whose tax liability to either Contracting State may be directly affected by a mutual agreement arising from that consideration. For example, a concerned person does not only include a U.S. corporation that brings a transfer pricing case with respect to a transaction entered into with its French subsidiary for resolution to the U.S. competent authority, but also the French subsidiary, which may have a correlative adjustment as a result of the resolution of the case.

Subparagraph 6(c) provides that an arbitration proceeding begins on the later of two dates: two years from the commencement date of that case, unless both competent authorities have previously agreed to a different date, or the earliest date upon which all concerned persons have entered into a confidentiality agreement and the agreements have been received by both competent authorities. The commencement date of the case is defined by subparagraph 6(b) as the earliest date on which the information necessary to undertake substantive consideration for a mutual agreement has been received by both competent authorities.

Clause p) of the Arbitration MOU provides that each competent authority will confirm in writing to the other competent authority and to the concerned persons the date of its receipt of the information necessary to undertake substantive consideration for a mutual agreement. Such information will be submitted to the competent authorities under relevant internal rules and procedures of each of the Contracting States. The information will not be considered received until both competent authorities have received copies of all materials submitted to either Contracting State by concerned persons in connection with the mutual agreement procedure.

The Arbitration MOU provides several procedural rules once an arbitration proceeding under paragraph 5 of Article 26 has commenced, but the competent authorities may complete these rules as necessary. In addition, the arbitration panel may adopt any procedures necessary for the conduct of its business, provided the procedures are not inconsistent with any provision of Article 26.

Clause e) of the Arbitration MOU provides that each Contracting State has 90 days from the date on which the arbitration proceeding begins to send a written communication to the other Contracting State appointing one member of the arbitration panel. The members of the arbitration panel shall not be employees of the tax administration which appoints them. Within 60 days of the date the second of such communications is sent, these two board members will appoint a third member to serve as the chair of the panel. The competent authorities will develop a non-exclusive list of individuals familiar in international tax matters who may potentially serve as the chair of the panel, but in any case, the chair can not be a citizen of either Contracting State. In the event that the two members appointed by the Contracting States fail to agree on the third member by the requisite date, these members will be dismissed and each Contracting State will appoint a new member of the panel within 30 days of the dismissal of the original members.

Clause g) of the Arbitration MOU establishes deadlines for submission of materials by the Contracting States to the arbitration panel. Each competent authority has 60 days from the date of appointment of the chair to submit a Proposed Resolution describing the proposed disposition of the specific monetary amounts of income, expense or taxation at issue in the case, and a supporting Position Paper. Copies of each State's submissions are to be provided by the panel to the other Contracting State on the date on which the later of the submissions is submitted to the panel. Each of the Contracting States may submit a Reply Submission to the panel within 120 days of the appointment of the chair to address points raised in the other State's Proposed Resolution or Position Paper. If one Contracting State fails to submit a Proposed Resolution within the requisite time, the Proposed Resolution of the other Contracting State is deemed to be the determination of the arbitration panel in the case and the arbitration proceeding will be terminated. Additional information may be supplied to the arbitration panel by a Contracting State only at the panel's request. The panel will provide copies of any such requested information, along with the panel's request, to the other Contracting State on the date on which the request or response is submitted. All communication from the Contracting States to the panel, and vice versa, is to be in writing between the chair of the panel and the designated competent authorities with the exception of communication regarding logistical matters.

Clause h) of the Arbitration MOU provides that the presenter of the case to the competent authority of a Contracting State may submit a Position Paper to the panel for consideration by the panel. The Position Paper must be submitted within 90 days of the appointment of the chair, and the panel will provide copies of the Position Paper to the Contracting States on the date on which the later of the submissions of the Contracting States is submitted to the panel.

The arbitration panel must deliver a determination in writing to the Contracting States within six months of the appointment of the chair. The determination must be one of the two Proposed Resolutions submitted by the Contracting States. The determination may only provide a determination regarding the amount of income, expense or tax reportable to the Contracting States. The determination has no precedential value and consequently the rationale behind a panel's determination would not be beneficial and may not be provided by the panel.

Unless any concerned person does not accept the decision of the arbitration panel, the determination of the panel constitutes a resolution by mutual agreement under Article 26 and, consequently, is binding on both Contracting States. Within 30 days of receiving the determination from the competent authority to which the case was first presented, each concerned person must advise that competent authority whether the person accepts the determination. In addition, if the case is in litigation, each concerned person who is a party to the litigation must also advise, within the same time frame, the court of its acceptance of the arbitration determination, and withdraw from the litigation the issues resolved by the arbitration proceeding. If any concerned person fails to advise the competent authority and relevant court within the requisite time, such failure is considered a rejection of the determination. If a determination is rejected, the case cannot be the subject of a subsequent arbitration proceeding. After the commencement of the arbitration proceeding but before a decision of the panel has been accepted by all concerned persons, the competent authorities may reach a mutual agreement to resolve the case and terminate the arbitration proceeding. Correspondingly, a concerned person may withdraw its request for the competent authorities to engage in the Mutual Agreement Procedure and thereby terminate the arbitration proceeding at any time.

For purposes of the arbitration proceeding, the members of the arbitration panel and their staffs shall be considered "persons or authorities" to whom information may be disclosed under Article 27 (Exchange of Information). Clause n) of the Arbitration MOU provides that all materials prepared in the course of, or relating to the arbitration proceeding are considered information exchanged between the Contracting States. No information relating to the arbitration proceeding or the panel's determination may be disclosed by members of the arbitration panel or their staffs or by either competent authority, except as permitted by the Convention and the domestic laws of the Contracting States. Members of the arbitration panel and their staffs must agree in statements sent to each of the Contracting States in confirmation of their appointment to the arbitration board to abide by and be subject to the confidentiality and nondisclosure provisions of Article 27 of the Convention and the applicable domestic laws of the Contracting States, with the most restrictive of the provisions applying.

The applicable domestic law of the Contracting States determines the treatment of any interest or penalties associated with a competent authority agreement achieved through arbitration.

Fees and expenses are borne equally by the Contracting States, including the cost of translation services. In general, the fees of members of the arbitration panel will be set at the fixed amount of $2,000 per day or the equivalent amount in euros. The expenses of members of the panel will be set in accordance with the International Centre for Settlement of Investment Disputes (ICSID) Schedule of Fees for arbitrators (in effect on the date on which the arbitration board proceedings begin). The competent authorities may amend the set fees and expenses of members of the board. Meeting facilities, related resources, financial management, other logistical support, and general and administrative coordination of the arbitration proceeding will be provided, at its own cost, by the Contracting State whose competent authority initiated the mutual agreement proceedings. All other costs are to be borne by the Contracting State that incurs them.

Article XI

Article XI of the Protocol replaces Article 27 (Exchange of Information) of the Convention. New paragraph 1 of Article 27 is substantially the same as the first two sentences of paragraph 1 of Article 27 of the existing Convention. The substance of the remaining two sentences of former paragraph 1 are found in new paragraph 2 of the Article, discussed below.

Paragraph 1 of Article 27

New paragraph 1 authorizes the competent authorities to exchange information as may be relevant for carrying out the provisions of the Convention or to the administration or enforcement of the domestic laws concerning taxes imposed by the Contracting States, insofar as the taxation under those domestic laws is not contrary to the Convention. New paragraph 1 uses the phrase "may be relevant", which is used in the U.S. Model, to clarify that the rule incorporates the standard in Code section 7602 which authorizes the Internal Revenue Service to examine "any books, papers, records, or other data which *may be relevant* or material." (Emphasis added.) In *United States v. Arthur Young & Co.*, 465 U.S. 805, 814 (1984), the Supreme Court stated that "the language 'may be' reflects Congress's express intention to allow the Internal Revenue Service to obtain 'items of even *potential* relevance to an ongoing investigation, without reference to its admissibility.'" (Emphasis in original.) However, the language "may be" would not support a request in which a Contracting State simply asked for information regarding all bank accounts maintained by residents of that Contracting State in the other Contracting State, or even all accounts maintained by its residents with respect to a particular bank.

The authority to exchange information granted by paragraph 1 is not restricted by Article 1 (Personal Scope) or Article 2 (Taxes Covered), and thus need not relate solely to persons or taxes otherwise covered by the Convention. For purposes of Article 27, the taxes covered by the Convention constitute a broader category of taxes than those referred to in Article 2 (Taxes Covered). Exchange of information is authorized with respect to taxes of every kind imposed by a Contracting State at the national level. Accordingly, information may be exchanged with respect to U.S. estate and gift taxes, excise taxes or, with respect to France, value added taxes. In this regard, paragraph 1 is broader than paragraph 1 of Article 27 of the 2004 Convention. Article 27 does not apply to taxes imposed by political subdivisions or local authorities of the Contracting States.

Paragraph 2 of Article 27

New paragraph 2 of Article 27 is substantially the same as the last two sentences of paragraph 1 of Article 27 of the existing Convention. Under paragraph 2, information may be exchanged for use in all phases of the taxation process including assessment, collection, enforcement or the determination of appeals. Thus, the competent authorities may request and provide information for cases under examination or criminal investigation, in collection, on appeals, or under prosecution.

Any information received by a Contracting State pursuant to the Convention is to be treated as secret in the same manner as information obtained under the tax laws of that State. Such information shall be disclosed only to persons or authorities, including courts and administrative bodies, involved in the assessment or collection of, the administration and enforcement in respect of, the determination of appeals in relation to the taxes referred to in new paragraph 1 of Article 27, or to the oversight of the above. The information may be used by such persons only for such purposes. Although the information received by persons described in paragraph 2 is to be treated as secret, it may be disclosed by such persons in public court proceedings or in judicial decisions.

The provisions of paragraph 2 authorize the U.S. competent authority to continue to allow legislative bodies, such as the tax-writing committees of Congress and the Government Accountability Office, to examine tax return information received from France when such bodies or offices are engaged in overseeing the administration of U.S. tax laws or a study of the administration of U.S. tax laws pursuant to a directive of Congress. However, the secrecy requirements of paragraph 2 must be met.

Paragraph 3 of Article 27

New paragraph 3 is substantively the same as paragraph 2 of Article 27 of the existing Convention. Paragraph 3 provides that the provisions of paragraphs 1 and 2 do not impose on France or the United States the obligation to carry out administrative measures at variance with the laws and administrative practice of either State; to supply information which is not obtainable under the laws or in the normal course of the administration of either State; or to supply information which would disclose any trade, business, industrial, commercial or professional secret or trade process, or information the disclosure of which would be contrary to public policy.

Thus, a requesting State may be denied information from the other State if the information would be obtained pursuant to procedures or measures that are broader than those available in the requesting State. However, the statute of limitations of the Contracting State making the request for information should govern a request for information. Thus, the Contracting State of which the request is made should attempt to obtain the information even if its own statute of limitations has passed. In many cases, relevant information will still exist in the business records of the taxpayer or a third party, even though it is no longer required to be kept for domestic tax purposes.

While paragraph 3 states conditions under which a Contracting State is not obligated to comply with a request from the other Contracting State for information, the requested State is not precluded from providing such information, and may, at its discretion, do so subject to the limitations of its internal law. In addition, as made clear by paragraph 4, in no case shall the limitations in paragraph 3 be construed to permit a Contracting State to decline to obtain information and supply information because it has no domestic tax interest in such information.

Paragraph 4 of Article 27

Subparagraph a) of paragraph 4 corresponds to paragraph 4 of Article 26 of the U.S. Model and provides that if a Contracting State requests information in accordance with Article 27, the other Contracting State shall use its information gathering measures to obtain the requested information. Subparagraph 4a) makes clear that the obligation to provide information is limited by the provisions of paragraph 3, but that such limitations shall not be construed to permit a Contracting State to decline to obtain and supply information because it has no domestic tax interest in such information. In the absence of such a provision, some taxpayers have argued that subparagraph 3a) prevents a Contracting State from requesting information from a bank or fiduciary that the Contracting State does not need for its own tax purposes. This paragraph clarifies that paragraph 3 does not impose such a restriction and that a Contracting State is not limited to providing only the information that it already has in its own files.

Subparagraph b) of new paragraph 4 is the same as subparagraph 4b) of Article 27 of the existing Convention and corresponds to paragraph 6 of Article 26 of the U.S. Model. Subparagraph 4b) provides that the requesting State may specify the form in which information to be provided, (*e.g.*, depositions of witnesses and authenticated copies of original documents). The intention is to ensure that the information may be introduced as evidence in the judicial proceedings of the requesting State. The requested State should, if possible, provide the information in the form requested to the same extent that it can obtain information in that form under its own laws and administrative practices with respect to its own taxes.

Subparagraph c) of new paragraph 4 is the same as subparagraph 4c) of Article 27 of the existing Convention and corresponds to paragraph 8 of Article 26 of the U.S. Model. Subparagraph 4c) provides that the requested State shall allow representatives of the requesting State to enter the requested State to interview taxpayers and look at and copy their books and records, but only after obtaining the consent of those taxpayers and the competent authority of the requested State, and only if the two States agree to allow such inquiries on a reciprocal basis. Such inquiries will not be considered audits for purposes of French domestic law. Subparagraph 4c) was intended to reinforce that the administrations can conduct consensual tax examinations abroad, and was not intended to limit travel or supersede any arrangements or procedures the competent authorities may have previously had in place regarding travel for tax administration purposes.

Paragraph 5 of Article 27

New paragraph 5 conforms with the corresponding U.S. and OECD Model provisions. Paragraph 5 provides that a Contracting State may not decline to provide information because that information is held by a financial institution, nominee or person acting in an agency or fiduciary capacity. Thus, paragraph 5 would effectively prevent a Contracting State from relying on paragraph 3 to argue that its domestic bank secrecy laws (or similar legislation relating to disclosure of financial information by financial institutions or intermediaries) override its obligation to provide information under paragraph 1. This paragraph also requires the disclosure of information regarding the beneficial owner of an interest in a person.

Article XII

Article XII of the Protocol replaces paragraph 5 of Article 28 (Assistance in Collection) of the Convention. The change revises paragraph 5 so as to remove the now obsolete reference to the provision of paragraph 4 of Article 10 (Dividends) of the existing Convention prior to amendment by the Protocol related to the "avoir fiscal."

Article XIII

Article XIII of the Protocol amends Article 29 (Miscellaneous Provisions) of the Convention.

Paragraph 1

Paragraph 1 replaces Paragraph 2 of Article 29 of the existing Convention. New paragraph 2 provides that notwithstanding any provision of the Convention except as provided in paragraph 3, the United States may tax its residents and citizens as if the Convention had not come into effect, and France may tax entities which have their place of effective management and which are subject to tax in France as if paragraph 3 of Article 4 of the Convention had not come into effect.

New paragraph 2 also contains language that corresponds to former paragraph 2, but revises certain language pertaining to former citizens and former long-term residents. These changes bring the Convention into conformity with the U.S. taxation of former citizens and long-term residents under Code section 877. Section 877 generally applies to a former citizen or long-term resident of the United States who relinquishes citizenship or terminates long-term residency before June 17, 2008 if he fails to certify that he has complied with U.S. tax laws during the 5 preceding years, or if either of the following criteria exceed established thresholds: (a) the average annual net income tax of such individual for the period of 5 taxable years ending before the date of the loss of status, or (b) the net worth of such individual as of the date of the loss of status.

The revised language of new paragraph 2 provides that a former citizen or former long-term resident of a Contracting State, may, for a period of ten years following the loss of such status, be taxed in accordance with the laws of the Contracting State with respect to its income from, or treated under the domestic laws of that Contracting State as being from, sources within that Contracting State. A "long term resident" is defined to mean, with respect to either Contracting State, any individual (other than a citizen of that Contracting State) who is a lawful permanent resident of that Contracting State in at least eight taxable years during the preceding fifteen taxable years. Paragraph 1 also provides that France may tax entities which have their place of effective management in France and which are subject to tax in France as if paragraph 3 of Article 4 (Residence) of the Convention had not come into effect.

Paragraph 2

Paragraph 2 revises paragraph 3(b) of Article 29 of the existing Convention so as to make the application of the exception to paragraph 2 of Article 29 bilateral, consistent with the bilateral application of the rules pertaining to former citizens and former long-term residents under paragraph 2 of Article 29 as revised by paragraph 1 of the Article.

Paragraph 3

Paragraph 3 updates the cross-references contained in paragraph 7(b) of Article 29 of the existing Convention to conform to the change in the paragraph numbering in Article 24 (Relief from Double Taxation) provided by paragraph 1 of Article VIII of the Protocol.

Paragraph 4

Paragraph 4 adds a new paragraph 9 to Article 29 of the existing Convention that overrides the rules of Article 19 (Public Remuneration) of the existing Convention in certain cases. Under paragraph 1(a) of Article 19 and paragraphs 2 and 3(b) of Article 29 of the existing Convention, remuneration, other than a pension, paid by France, a local authority thereof, or an agency or instrumentality of France or a local authority thereof (collectively the French government), to a lawful permanent resident (green card holder) of the United States, whether or not a national of France, for services provided to the French government in the United States is taxable in both France and the United States. Double taxation is relieved under paragraph 1 of Article 24 (Relief from Double Taxation). See also Announcement 97-61, 1997-29 I.R.B. 13 (extending the resourcing rule of Article 24(1)(c) to green card holders). This can result in some double taxation if the limitations of the law of the United States disallow credit for some of the French tax. New paragraph 9 of Article 29 remedies this problem by providing that remuneration paid by the French government to green card holders working for the French government in the United States will be taxable only in the United States. The new paragraph also provides that remuneration paid by the French government to nationals and residents of the United States for services provided to the French government in the United States will be taxable only in the United States even if the service provider is also a national of France. Under the existing Convention, such remuneration is exempt from U.S. tax if the service provider is a national of both countries.

Article XIV

Article XIV of the Protocol replaces Article 30 (Limitation on Benefits of the Convention) of the Convention. Article 30 contains anti-treaty-shopping provisions that are intended to prevent residents of third countries from benefiting from what is intended to be a reciprocal agreement between two countries. In general, the provision does not rely on a determination of purpose or intention but instead sets forth a series of objective tests. A resident of a Contracting State that satisfies one of the tests will receive benefits regardless of its motivations in choosing its particular business structure.

The structure of the Article is as follows: Paragraph 1 states the general rule that a resident of a Contracting State is entitled to benefits otherwise accorded to residents only to the extent provided in the Article. Paragraph 2 lists a series of attributes of a resident of a Contracting State, the presence of any one of which will entitle that person to all the benefits of the Convention. Paragraph 3 provides a so-called "derivative benefits" test under which certain categories of income may qualify for benefits. Paragraph 4 sets forth the "active trade or business test," under which a person may be granted benefits with regard to certain types of income regardless of whether the person qualifies for benefits under paragraph 2. Paragraph 5 provides special rules for so-called "triangular cases" notwithstanding the other provisions of Article 30. Paragraph 6 provides that benefits may also be granted if the competent authority of the State from which the benefits are claimed determines that it is appropriate to provide benefits in that case. Paragraph 7 defines certain terms used in the Article.

Paragraph 1 of Article 30

Paragraph 1 provides that a resident of a Contracting State is entitled to all the benefits of the Convention otherwise accorded to residents of a Contracting State only to the extent provided in the Article. The benefits otherwise accorded to residents under the Convention include all limitations on source-based taxation under Articles 6 (Income from Real Property) through 23 (Capital), the treaty-based relief from double taxation provided by Article 24 (Relief from Double Taxation), and the protection afforded to residents of a Contracting State under Article 25 (Nondiscrimination). Some provisions do not require that a person be a resident in order to enjoy the benefits of those provisions. For example, Article 26 (Mutual Agreement Procedure) is not limited to residents of the Contracting States, and Article 31 (Diplomatic and Consular Officers) applies to diplomatic agents and consular officers regardless of residence. Article 30 accordingly does not limit the availability of treaty benefits under such provisions.

Article 30 and the anti-abuse provisions of domestic law complement each other, as Article 30 effectively determines whether an entity has a sufficient nexus to a Contracting State to be treated as a resident for treaty purposes, while domestic anti-abuse provisions (*e.g.*, business purpose, substance-over-form, step transaction or conduit principles) determine whether a particular transaction should be recast in accordance with its substance. Thus, internal law principles of the source Contracting State may be applied to identify the beneficial owner of an item of income, and Article 30 then will be applied to the beneficial owner to determine if that person is entitled to the benefits of the Convention with respect to such income.

Paragraph 2 of Article 30

Paragraph 2 has six subparagraphs, each of which describes a category of residents that are entitled to all benefits of the Convention. It is intended that the provisions of paragraph 2 will be self-executing. Unlike the provisions of paragraph 6, discussed below, claiming benefits under paragraph 2 does not require an advance competent authority ruling or approval. The tax authorities may, of course, on review, determine that the taxpayer has improperly interpreted the paragraph and is not entitled to the benefits claimed.

Individuals -- Subparagraph 2(a)

Subparagraph 2(a) provides that individual residents of a Contracting State will be entitled to all the benefits of the Convention. If such an individual receives income as a nominee on behalf of a third country resident, benefits may be denied under the applicable articles of the Convention by the requirement that the beneficial owner of the income be a resident of a Contracting State.

Governments -- Subparagraph 2(b)

Subparagraph 2(b) provides that the Contracting States and any political subdivision or local authority thereof will be entitled to all the benefits of the Convention.

Publicly-Traded Corporations -- Subparagraph 2(c)(i)

Subparagraph 2(c) applies to two categories of companies: publicly traded companies and subsidiaries of publicly traded companies. A company resident in a Contracting State is entitled to all the benefits of the Convention under clause (i) of subparagraph 2(c) if the principal class of its shares, and any disproportionate class of shares, is regularly traded on one or more recognized stock exchanges and the company satisfies at least one of the following additional tests. First, the company's principal class of shares is primarily traded on a recognized stock exchange located in a Contracting State of which the company is a resident (or, in the case of a company resident in France, on a recognized stock exchange located within the European Union or, in the case of a company resident in the United States, on a recognized stock exchange located in another state that is a party to the North American Free Trade Agreement). Second, the company's primary place of management and control is in its State of residence.

The term "recognized stock exchange" is defined in subparagraph (d) of paragraph 7. It includes (i) the NASDAQ System and any stock exchange registered with the Securities and Exchange Commission as a national securities exchange for purposes of the Securities Exchange Act of 1934; (ii) the French stock exchanges controlled by the "Autorité des marchés financiers"; (iii) the stock exchanges of Amsterdam, Brussels, Frankfurt, Hamburg, London, Lisbon, Madrid, Milan, Stockholm, Sydney, Tokyo, Toronto and the Swiss stock exchange; and (iv) any other stock exchange agreed upon by the competent authorities of the Contracting States.

If a company has only one class of shares, it is only necessary to consider whether the shares of that class meet the relevant trading requirements. If the company has more than one class of shares, it is necessary as an initial matter to determine which class or classes constitute the "principal class of shares." The term "principal class of shares" is defined in subparagraph (a) of paragraph 7 to mean the ordinary or common shares of the company representing the majority of the aggregate voting power and value of the company. If the company does not have a class of ordinary or common shares representing the majority of the aggregate voting power and value of the company, then the "principal class of shares" is that class or any combination of classes of shares that represents, in the aggregate, a majority of the voting power and value of the company. Although in a particular case involving a company with several classes of shares it is conceivable that more than one group of classes could be identified that account for more than 50 percent of the shares, it is only necessary for one such group to satisfy the requirements of this subparagraph in order for the company to be entitled to benefits. Benefits would not be denied to the company even if a second, non-qualifying, group of shares with more than half of the company's voting power and value could be identified. Subparagraph (c) of paragraph 7 defines the term "shares" to include depository receipts for shares.

A company whose principal class of shares is regularly traded on a recognized stock exchange will nevertheless not qualify for benefits under subparagraph (c) of paragraph 2 if it has a disproportionate class of shares that is not regularly traded on a recognized stock exchange. The term "disproportionate class of shares" is defined in subparagraph (b) of paragraph 7. A company has a disproportionate class of shares if it has outstanding a class of shares that is subject to terms or other arrangements that entitle the holder to a larger portion of the company's income, profit, or gain in the other Contracting State than that to which the holder would be entitled in the absence of such terms or arrangements. Thus, for example, a company resident in France has a disproportionate class of shares if it has outstanding a class of "tracking stock" that pays dividends based upon a formula that approximates the company's return on its assets employed in the United States.

The following example illustrates this result.

Example. FCo is a corporation resident in France. FCo has two classes of shares: Common and Preferred. The Common shares are listed and regularly traded on a designated stock exchange in France. The Preferred shares have no voting rights and are entitled to receive dividends equal in amount to interest payments that FCo receives from unrelated borrowers in the United States. The Preferred shares are owned entirely by a single investor that is a resident of a country with which the United States does not have a tax treaty. The Common shares account for more than 50 percent of the value of FCo and for 100 percent of the voting power. Because the owner of the Preferred shares is entitled to receive payments corresponding to the U.S. source interest income earned by FCo, the Preferred shares are a disproportionate class of shares. Because the Preferred shares are not regularly traded on a recognized stock exchange, FCo will not qualify for benefits under subparagraph (c) of paragraph 2.

The term "regularly traded" is not defined in the Convention. In accordance with paragraph 2 of Article 3 (General Definitions), this term will be defined by reference to the domestic laws of the State from which treaty benefits are sought, generally the Source State. In the case of the United States, this term is understood to have the meaning it has under Treas. Reg. section 1.884-5(d)(4)(i)(B), relating to the branch tax provisions of the

Code. Under these regulations, a class of shares is considered to be "regularly traded" if two requirements are met: trades in the class of shares are made in more than *de minimis* quantities on at least 60 days during the taxable year, and the aggregate number of shares in the class traded during the year is at least 10 percent of the average number of shares outstanding during the year. Section 1.884-5(d)(4)(i)(A), (ii) and (iii) will not be taken into account for purposes of defining the term "regularly traded" under the Convention.

The regularly traded requirement can be met by trading on any recognized exchange or exchanges. Trading on one or more recognized stock exchanges may be aggregated for purposes of this requirement. Thus, a U.S. company could satisfy the regularly traded requirement through trading, in whole or in part, on a recognized stock exchange located in France. Authorized but unissued shares are not considered for purposes of this test.

The term "primarily traded" is not defined in the Convention. In accordance with paragraph 2 of Article 3, this term will have the meaning it has under the laws of the State concerning the taxes to which the Convention applies, generally the source State. In the case of the United States, this term is understood to have the meaning it has under Treas. Reg. section 1.884-5(d)(3), relating to the branch tax provisions of the Code. Accordingly, stock of a corporation is "primarily traded" if the number of shares in the company's principal class of shares that are traded during the taxable year on all recognized stock exchanges in the Contracting State of which the company is a resident exceeds the number of shares in the company's principal class of shares that are traded during that year on established securities markets in any other single foreign country.

A company whose principal class of shares is regularly traded on a recognized exchange but cannot meet the primarily traded test may claim treaty benefits if its primary place of management and control is in its country of residence. This test should be distinguished from the "place of effective management" test which is used in the OECD Model and by many other countries to establish residence. In some cases, the place of effective management test has been interpreted to mean the place where the board of directors meets. By contrast, the primary place of management and control test looks to where day-to-day responsibility for the management of the company (and its subsidiaries) is exercised. The company's primary place of management and control will be located in the State in which the company is a resident only if the executive officers and senior management employees exercise day-to-day responsibility for more of the strategic, financial and operational policy decision making for the company (including direct and indirect subsidiaries) in that State than in the other State or any third state, and the staff that support the management in making those decisions are also based in that State. Thus, the test looks to the overall activities of the relevant persons to see where those activities are conducted. In most cases, it will be a necessary, but not a sufficient, condition that the headquarters of the company (that is, the place at which the Chief Executive Officer and other top executives normally are based) be located in the Contracting State of which the company is a resident.

To apply the test, it will be necessary to determine which persons are to be considered "executive officers and senior management employees". In most cases, it will not be necessary to look beyond the executives who are members of the Board of Directors (the "inside directors") in the case of a U.S. company. That will not always be the case, however; in fact, the relevant persons may be employees of subsidiaries if those persons make the strategic, financial and operational policy decisions. Moreover, it would be necessary to take into account any special voting arrangements that result in certain board members making certain decisions without the participation of other board members.

Subsidiaries of Publicly-Traded Corporations -- Subparagraph 2(c)(ii)

A company resident in a Contracting State is entitled to all the benefits of the Convention under clause (ii) of subparagraph (c) of paragraph 2 if five or fewer publicly traded companies described in clause (i) are the direct or indirect owners of at least 50 percent of the aggregate vote and value of the company's shares (and at least 50 percent of any disproportionate class of shares). If the publicly-traded companies are indirect owners, however, each of the intermediate companies must be a resident of one of the Contracting States.

Thus, for example, a company that is a resident of France, all the shares of which are owned by another company that is a resident of France, would qualify for benefits under the Convention if the principal class of shares (and any disproportionate classes of shares) of the parent company are regularly and primarily traded on a recognized stock exchange in France. However, such a subsidiary would not qualify for benefits under clause (ii) if the publicly traded parent company were a resident of a third state, for example, and not a resident of the United States or France. Furthermore, if a French parent company indirectly owned the bottom-tier company through a chain of subsidiaries, each such subsidiary in the chain, as an intermediate owner, must be a resident of the United States or France for the subsidiary to meet the test in clause (ii).

Pension Trusts and Tax-Exempt Organizations -- Subparagraph 2(d)

Subparagraph 2(d) provides rules by which the pension trusts and tax exempt organizations described in clause (ii) of subparagraph (b) of paragraph 2 of Article 4 (Resident) will be entitled to all the benefits of the Convention. A pension trust and any other organization established in a Contracting State and maintained exclusively to administer or provide retirement benefits that is established or sponsored by a person that is a resident of that State under the provisions of Article 4 will qualify for benefits if more than 50 percent of the person's beneficiaries, members or participants are individuals resident in either Contracting State, or the organization sponsoring such person is entitled to benefits under the Convention (*i.e.*, meets the limitations on benefits provisions of Article 30). For purposes of this provision, the term "beneficiaries" should be understood to refer to the persons receiving benefits from the pension trust. On the other hand, a not-for-profit organization other than a pensions trust that is resident in a Contracting State automatically qualifies for benefits, without regard to the residence of its beneficiaries or members. Entities qualifying under this rule are those that are generally exempt from tax in their State of residence and that are established and maintained exclusively for religious, charitable, educational, scientific, artistic or cultural purposes.

Ownership/Base Erosion -- Subparagraph 2(e)

Subparagraph 2(e) provides an additional method to qualify for treaty benefits that applies to any form of legal entity that is a resident of a Contracting State. The test provided in subparagraph 2(e), the so-called ownership and base erosion test, is a two-part test. Both prongs of the test must be satisfied for the resident to be entitled to treaty benefits under subparagraph 2(f).

The ownership prong of the test, under clause (i), requires that 50 percent or more of each class of shares or other beneficial interests in the person is owned, directly or indirectly, on at least half the days of the person's taxable year by persons who are residents of the Contracting State of which the person claiming benefits is a resident and that are themselves entitled to treaty benefits under subparagraphs 2(a), (b), (d), or clause (i) of subparagraph 2(c). In the case of indirect owners, however, each of the intermediate owners must be a resident of that Contracting State.

Trusts may be entitled to benefits under this provision if they are treated as residents under Article 4 (Resident) and they otherwise satisfy the requirements of this subparagraph. For purposes of this subparagraph, the beneficial interests in a trust will be considered to be owned by its beneficiaries in proportion to each beneficiary's actuarial interest in the trust. The interest of a remainder beneficiary will be equal to 100 percent less the aggregate percentages held by income beneficiaries. A beneficiary's interest in a trust will not be considered to be owned by a person entitled to benefits under subparagraph 2(a), 2(b), 2(d) or clause (i) of subparagraph 2(c) if it is not possible to determine the beneficiary's actuarial interest. Consequently, if it is not possible to determine the actuarial interest of the beneficiaries in a trust, the ownership test under clause (i) cannot be satisfied, unless all possible beneficiaries are persons entitled to benefits under subparagraph 2(a), 2(b), 2(d) or clause (i) of subparagraph 2(c).

The base erosion prong of clause (ii) of subparagraph (e) is satisfied with respect to a person if less than 50 percent of the person's gross income for the taxable year, as determined under the tax law in the person's State of residence, is paid or accrued, directly or indirectly, to persons who are not residents of either Contracting State entitled to benefits under subparagraph 2(a), 2(b), 2(d) or clause (i) of subparagraph 2(c), in the form of payments deductible for tax purposes in the payor's State of residence. These amounts do not include arm's length payments in the ordinary course of business for services or tangible property, or payments in respect of financial obligations to a bank that is not related to the payor. To the extent they are deductible from the taxable base, trust distributions are deductible payments. However, depreciation and amortization deductions, which do not represent payments or accruals to other persons, are disregarded for this purpose.

Investment entities -- Subparagraph 2(f)

Subparagraph 2(f) provides a rule by which investment entities described in clause (iii) of subparagraph (b) of paragraph 2 of Article 4 (Resident) will be entitled to all the benefits of the Convention. Such an entity will qualify for benefits if more than half of the shares, rights, or interests in such entity are owned directly or indirectly by persons that are resident of the same State of which the investment entity is a resident and that qualify for benefits under subparagraph 2(a), 2(b), 2(d) or clause (i) of subparagraph 2(c), and U.S. citizens in the case of an investment entity that is a resident of the United States. In the case of indirect ownership, each intermediate owner must be a resident of the Contracting State of which the investment entity is a resident.

Paragraph 3 of Article 30

Paragraph 3 sets forth a derivative benefits test that is potentially applicable to all treaty benefits, although the test is applied to individual items of income. In general, a derivative benefits test entitles the resident of a Contracting State to treaty benefits if the owner of the resident would have been entitled to the same benefit had the income in question flowed directly to that owner. To qualify under this paragraph, the company must meet an ownership test and a base erosion test.

Subparagraph (a) sets forth the ownership test. Under this test, at least 95 percent of the aggregate voting power and value of the company and at least 50 percent of any disproportionate class of shares must be owned by seven or fewer persons that are "equivalent beneficiaries" as defined in subparagraph 7(f). This definition may be met in two alternative ways.

Under the first alternative, a person may be treated as a resident of a member state of the European Union or of a party to the North American Free Trade Agreement because it is entitled to equivalent benefits under a treaty between the country of source and the country in which the person is a resident. To satisfy this requirement, the person must be entitled to all the benefits of a comprehensive treaty between the Contracting State from which benefits of the Convention are claimed and a qualifying State under provisions that are analogous to the rules in subparagraph 2(a), 2(b), 2(d), and clause (i) of subparagraph 2(c). If the treaty in question does not have a comprehensive limitation on benefits article, this requirement is met only if the person would be entitled to treaty benefits under the tests in subparagraphs 2(a), 2(b), 2(d), and clause (i) of subparagraph 2(c) of this Article if the person were a resident of one of the Contracting States.

In order to satisfy the first alternative with respect to insurance premiums, dividends, interest, royalties, or branch tax, paragraph 7(f)(i)(bb) provides that the person must be entitled to a rate of tax that is at least as low as the tax rate that would apply under the Convention to such income. Thus, the rates to be compared are: (1) the rate of tax that the source State would have imposed if a qualified resident of the other Contracting State was the beneficial owner of the income; and (2) the rate of tax that the source State would have imposed if the third State resident received the income directly from the source State. For example, USCo is a wholly owned subsidiary of FCo, a company resident in France. FCo is wholly owned by ICo, a corporation resident in Italy. Assuming FCo satisfies the requirements of paragraph 2 of Article 10 (Dividends), FCo would be eligible for a dividend withholding tax rate of 5 percent. The dividend withholding tax rate in the treaty between the United States and Italy is 5 percent. Thus, if ICo received the dividend directly from USCo, ICo would have been subject to a 5 percent rate of withholding tax on the dividend. Because ICo would be entitled to a rate of withholding tax that is at least as low as the rate that would apply under the Convention to such income, ICo is treated as a resident of a member state of the European Union or a party to the North American Free Trade Agreement with respect to the withholding tax on dividends.

Subparagraph 7(g) provides a special rule to take account of the fact that withholding taxes on many inter-company dividends, interest and royalties are exempt within the European Union by reason of various EU directives, rather than by tax treaty. If a U.S. company receives such payments from a French company, and that U.S. company is owned by a company resident in a member state of the European Union that would have qualified for an exemption from withholding tax if it had received the income directly, the parent company will be treated as an equivalent beneficiary. This rule is necessary because many European Union member countries have not re-negotiated their tax treaties to reflect the rates applicable under the directives.

The requirement that a person be entitled to "all the benefits" of a comprehensive tax treaty eliminates those persons that qualify for benefits with respect to only certain types of income. Accordingly, the fact that a Belgian parent of a French company is engaged in the active conduct of a trade or business in Belgium and therefore would be entitled to the benefits of the U.S.-Belgium treaty if it received dividends directly from a U.S. subsidiary of the French company is not sufficient for purposes of this paragraph. Further, the Belgian company cannot be an equivalent beneficiary if it itself qualifies for benefits only with respect to certain income as a result of a "derivative benefits" provision in the U.S.-Belgium treaty. However, it would be possible to look through the Belgian company to its parent company to determine whether the parent company is an equivalent beneficiary.

The second alternative for satisfying the "equivalent beneficiary" test is available only to residents of one of the two Contracting States. U.S. or French residents who are eligible for treaty benefits by reason of subparagraphs (a), (b), (d), or clause (i) of subparagraph (c) of paragraph 2 are equivalent beneficiaries under the second alternative. Thus, a French individual will be an equivalent beneficiary without regard to whether the individual would have been entitled to receive the same benefits if it received the income directly. A resident of a third country cannot qualify for treaty benefits under any of those subparagraphs or any other rule of the treaty, and therefore would not qualify as an equivalent beneficiary under this alternative. Thus, a resident of a third country can be an equivalent beneficiary only if it would have been entitled to equivalent benefits had it received the income directly.

The second alternative was included in order to clarify that ownership by certain residents of a Contracting State would not disqualify a U.S. or French company under this paragraph. Thus, for example, if 90 percent of a French company is owned by five companies that are resident in member states of the European Union who satisfy the requirements of clause (i) of subparagraph 8(f), and 10 percent of the French company is owned by a U.S. or French individual, then the French company still can satisfy the requirements of subparagraph (a) of paragraph 3.

Subparagraph (b) of paragraph 3 sets forth the base erosion test. A company meets this base erosion test if less than 50 percent of its gross income, as determined under the tax law in the company's State of residence, for the taxable period is paid or accrued, directly or indirectly, to a person or persons who are not equivalent beneficiaries in the form of payments deductible for tax purposes in the company's State of residence. This test is the same as the base erosion test in clause (ii) of subparagraph (e) of paragraph 2, except that the test in subparagraph 3(b) focuses on base-eroding payments to persons who are not equivalent beneficiaries.

As in the case of the base erosion test in subparagraph 2(e), deductible payments in subparagraph 3(b) also do not include arm's length payments in the ordinary course of business for services or tangible property and payments in respect of financial obligations to a bank that is not related to the payor.

Paragraph 4 of Article 30

Paragraph 4 sets forth an alternative test under which a resident of a Contracting State may receive treaty benefits with respect to certain items of income that are connected to an active trade or business conducted in its State of residence. A resident of a Contracting State may qualify for benefits under paragraph 4 whether or not it also qualifies under paragraph 2 or 3.

Subparagraph (a) sets forth the general rule that a resident of a Contracting State engaged in the active conduct of a trade or business in that State may obtain the benefits of the Convention with respect to an item of income derived from the other Contracting State. The item of income, however, must be derived in connection with or incidental to that trade or business.

The term "trade or business" is not defined in the Convention. Pursuant to paragraph 2 of Article 3 (General Definitions), when determining whether a resident of the France is entitled to the benefits of the Convention under paragraph 4 of this Article with respect to an item of income derived from sources within the United States, the United States will ascribe to this term the meaning that it has under the law of the United States. Accordingly, the U.S. competent authority will refer to the regulations issued under section 367(a) for the definition of the term "trade or business." In general, therefore, a trade or business will be considered to be a specific unified group of activities that constitute or could constitute an independent economic enterprise carried on for profit. Furthermore, a corporation generally will be considered to carry on a trade or business only if the officers and employees of the corporation conduct substantial managerial and operational activities.

The business of making or managing investments for the resident's own account will be considered to be a trade or business only when part of banking, insurance or securities activities conducted by a bank, an insurance company, or a registered securities dealer. Such activities conducted by a person other than a bank, insurance company or registered securities dealer will not be considered to be the conduct of an active trade or business, nor would they be considered to be the conduct of an active trade or business if conducted by a bank, insurance company or registered securities dealer but not as part of the company's banking, insurance or dealer business. Because a headquarters operation is in the business of managing investments, a company that functions solely as a headquarters company will not be considered to be engaged in an active trade or business for purposes of paragraph 4.

An item of income is derived in connection with a trade or business if the income-producing activity in the State of source is a line of business that "forms a part of" or is "complementary" to the trade or business conducted in the State of residence by the income recipient.

A business activity generally will be considered to form part of a business activity conducted in the State of source if the two activities involve the design, manufacture or sale of the same products or type of products, or the provision of similar services. The line of business in the State of residence may be upstream, downstream, or parallel to the activity conducted in the State of source. Thus, the line of business may provide inputs for a manufacturing process that occurs in the State of source, may sell the output of that manufacturing process, or simply may sell the same sorts of products that are being sold by the trade or business carried on in the State of source.

Example 1. USCo is a corporation resident in the United States. USCo is engaged in an active manufacturing business in the United States. USCo owns 100 percent of the shares of FCo, a company resident in France. FCo distributes USCo products in France. Because the business activities conducted by the two corporations involve the same products, FCo's distribution business is considered to form a part of USCo's manufacturing business.

Example 2. The facts are the same as in Example 1, except that USCo does not manufacture. Rather, USCo operates a large research and development facility in the United States that licenses intellectual property to affiliates worldwide, including FCo. FCo and other USCo affiliates then manufacture and market the USCo-designed products in their respective markets. Because the activities conducted by FCo and USCo involve the same product lines, these activities are considered to form a part of the same trade or business.

For two activities to be considered to be "complementary," the activities need not relate to the same types of products or services, but they should be part of the same overall industry and be related in the sense that the success or failure of one activity will tend to result in success or failure for the other. Where more than one trade or business is conducted in the State of source and only one of the trades or businesses forms a part of or is complementary to a trade or business conducted in the State of residence, it is necessary to identify the trade or business to which an item of income is attributable. Royalties generally will be considered to be derived in connection with the trade or business to which the underlying intangible property is attributable. Dividends will be deemed to be derived first out of earnings and profits of the treaty-benefited trade or business, and then out of other earnings and profits. Interest income may be allocated under any reasonable method consistently applied. A method that conforms to U.S. principles for expense allocation will be considered a reasonable method.

Example 3. Americair is a corporation resident in the United States that operates an international airline. FSub is a wholly-owned subsidiary of Americair resident in France. SSub operates a chain of hotels in France that are located near airports served by Americair flights. Americair frequently sells tour packages that include air travel to France and lodging at FSub hotels. Although both companies are engaged in the active conduct of a trade or business, the businesses of operating a chain of hotels and operating an airline are distinct trades or businesses. Therefore FSub's business does not form a part of Americair's business. However, FSub's business is considered to be complementary to Americair's business because they are part of the same overall industry (travel), and the links between their operations tend to make them interdependent.

Example 4. The facts are the same as in Example 3, except that FSub owns an office building in France instead of a hotel chain. No part of Americair's business is conducted through the office building. FSub's business is not considered to form a part of or to be complementary to Americair's business. They are engaged in distinct trades or businesses in separate industries, and there is no economic dependence between the two operations.

Example 5. USFlower is a company resident in the United States. USFlower produces and sells flowers in the United States and other countries. USFlower owns all the shares of FHolding, a corporation resident in France. FHolding is a holding company that is not engaged in a trade or business. FHolding owns all the shares of three corporations that are resident in France: FFlower, FLawn, and FFish. FFlower distributes USFlower flowers under the USFlower trademark in France. FLawn markets a line of lawn care products in France under the USFlower trademark. In addition to being sold under the same trademark, FLawn and FFlower products are sold in the same stores and sales of each company's products tend to generate increased sales of the other's products. FFish imports fish from the United States and distributes it to fish wholesalers in France. For purposes of paragraph 4, the business of FFlower forms a part of the business of USFlower, the business of FLawn is complementary to the business of USFlower, and the business of FFish is neither part of nor complementary to that of USFlower.

An item of income derived from the State of source is "incidental to" the trade or business carried on in the State of residence if production of the item facilitates the conduct of the trade or business in the State of residence. An example of incidental income is the temporary investment of working capital of a person in the State of residence in securities issued by persons in the State of source.

Subparagraph (b) of paragraph 4 states a further condition to the general rule in subparagraph (a) in cases where the trade or business generating the item of income in question is carried on either by the person deriving the income or by any associated enterprises. Subparagraph (b) states that the trade or business carried on in the State of residence, under these circumstances, must be substantial in relation to the activity in the State of source. The substantiality requirement is intended to prevent a narrow case of treaty-shopping abuses in which a company attempts to qualify for benefits by engaging in de minimis connected business activities in the treaty country in which it is resident (*i.e.*, activities that have little economic cost or effect with respect to the company business as a whole).

The determination of substantiality is made based upon all the facts and circumstances and takes into account the comparative sizes of the trades or businesses in each Contracting State , the nature of the activities performed in each Contracting State, and the relative contributions made to that trade or business in each Contracting State. In any case, in making each determination or comparison, due regard will be given to the relative sizes of the U.S. and French economies.

The determination in subparagraph 4(b) also is made separately for each item of income derived from the State of source. It therefore is possible that a person would be entitled to the benefits of the Convention with respect to one item of income but not with respect to another. If a resident of a Contracting State is entitled to treaty benefits with respect to a particular item of income under paragraph 4, the resident is entitled to all benefits of the Convention insofar as they affect the taxation of that item of income in the State of source.

The application of the substantiality requirement only to income from related parties focuses only on potential abuse cases, and does not hamper certain other kinds of non-abusive activities, even though the income recipient resident in a Contracting State may be very small in relation to the entity generating income in the other Contracting State. For example, if a small U.S. research firm develops a process that it licenses to a very large, unrelated, French pharmaceutical manufacturer, the size of the U.S. research firm would not have to be tested against the size of the French manufacturer. Similarly, a small U.S. bank that makes a loan to a very large unrelated French business would not have to pass a substantiality test to receive treaty benefits under paragraph 4.

Subparagraph (c) of paragraph 4 provides special attribution rules for purposes of applying the substantive rules of subparagraphs (a) and (b). Thus, these rules apply for purposes of determining whether a person meets the requirement in subparagraph (a) that it be engaged in the active conduct of a trade or business and that the item of income is derived in connection with that active trade or business, and for making the comparison required by the "substantiality" requirement in subparagraph (b). Subparagraph (c) attributes to a person activities conducted by a partnership in which that person is a partner. Subparagraph (c) also attributes to a person activities conducted by persons "connected" to such person. A person ("X") is connected to another person ("Y") if X possesses 50 percent or more of the beneficial interest in Y (or if Y possesses 50 percent or more of the beneficial interest in X). For this purpose, X is connected to a company if X owns shares representing fifty percent or more of the aggregate voting power and value of the company or fifty percent or more of the beneficial equity interest in the company. X also is connected to Y if a third person possesses fifty percent or more of the beneficial interest in both X and Y. For this purpose, if X or Y is a company, the threshold relationship with respect to such company or companies is fifty percent or more of the aggregate voting power and value or fifty percent or more of the beneficial equity interest. Finally, X is connected to Y if, based upon all the facts and circumstances, X controls Y, Y controls X, or X and Y are controlled by the same person or persons.

Paragraph 5 of Article 30

Paragraph 5 deals with the treatment of income in the context of a so-called "triangular case."

An example of a triangular case would be a structure under which a resident of France earns interest income from the United States. The resident of France, who is assumed to qualify for benefits under one or more of the provisions of Article 30, sets up a permanent establishment in a third jurisdiction that imposes only a low rate of tax on the income of the permanent establishment. The French resident lends funds into the United States through the permanent establishment. The permanent establishment, despite its third-jurisdiction location, is an integral part of a French resident. Therefore the income that it earns on those loans, absent the provisions of paragraph 5, is entitled to exemption from U.S. withholding tax under the Convention. Under a current French income tax treaty with the host jurisdiction of the permanent establishment, the income of the permanent establishment is exempt from French tax (alternatively, France may choose to exempt the income of the permanent establishment from French income tax by statute). Thus, the interest income is exempt from U.S. tax, is subject to little tax in the host jurisdiction of the permanent establishment, and is exempt from French tax.

Paragraph 5 applies reciprocally. However, the United States does not exempt the profits of a third-jurisdiction permanent establishment of a U.S. resident from U.S. tax, either by statute or by treaty.

Paragraph 5 provides that the tax benefits that would otherwise apply under the Convention will not apply to any item of income if the combined tax actually paid in the residence State and the third state is less than 60 percent of the tax that would have been payable in the residence State if the income were earned in that State by the enterprise and were not attributable to the permanent establishment in the third state. In the case of dividends, interest and royalties to which this paragraph applies, the withholding tax rates under the Convention are replaced with a 15 percent withholding tax. Any other income to which the provisions of paragraph 5 apply is subject to tax under the domestic law of the source State, notwithstanding any other provisions of the Convention.

In general, the principles employed under Code section 954(b)(4) will be employed to determine whether the profits are subject to an effective rate of taxation that is above the specified threshold.

Notwithstanding the level of tax on income of the permanent establishment, paragraph 5 will not apply under certain circumstances. In the case of royalties, paragraph 5 will not apply if the royalties are received as compensation for the use of, or the right to use, intangible property produced or developed by the permanent establishment itself. In the case of any other income, paragraph 5 will not apply if that income is derived in connection with, or is incidental to, the active conduct of a trade or business carried on by the permanent establishment in the third state. The business of making, managing or simply holding investments is not considered to be an active trade or business, unless these are banking or securities activities carried on by a bank or registered securities dealer.

Paragraph 6 of Article 30

Paragraph 6 provides that a resident of one of the Contracting States that is not entitled to the benefits of the Convention as a result of paragraphs 1 through 5 still shall be granted benefits under the Convention if the competent authority of the State from which benefits are claimed determines that the establishment, acquisition or maintenance of such person and the conduct of its operations did not have as one of its principal purposes the obtaining of benefits under the Convention. Benefits will not be granted, however, solely because a company was established prior to the effective date of a treaty or protocol. In that case a company would still be required to establish to the satisfaction of the Competent Authority clear non-tax business reasons for its formation in a Contracting State, or that the allowance of benefits would not otherwise be contrary to the purposes of the treaty. Thus, persons that establish operations in one of the States with a principal purpose of obtaining the benefits of the Convention ordinarily will not be granted relief under paragraph 6.

The competent authority's discretion is quite broad. It may grant all of the benefits of the Convention to the taxpayer making the request, or it may grant only certain benefits. For instance, it may grant benefits only with respect to a particular item of income in a manner similar to paragraph 4. Further, the competent authority may establish conditions, such as setting time limits on the duration of any relief granted.

For purposes of implementing paragraph 6, a taxpayer will be permitted to present his case to the relevant competent authority for an advance determination based on the facts. In these circumstances, it is also expected that, if the competent authority determines that benefits are to be allowed, they will be allowed retroactively to the time of entry into force of the relevant treaty provision or the establishment of the structure in question, whichever is later. Before denying benefits of the Convention under this paragraph, the competent authority will consult with the competent authority of the other Contracting State.

Finally, there may be cases in which a resident of a Contracting State may apply for discretionary relief to the competent authority of his State of residence. This would arise, for example, if the benefit it is claiming is provided by the residence country, and not by the source country. So, for example, if a company that is a resident of the United States would like to claim the benefit of the re-sourcing rule of paragraph 2 of Article 24, but it does not meet any of the objective tests of this Article, it may apply to the U.S. competent authority for discretionary relief.

Paragraph 7 of Article 30

Paragraph 7 defines several key terms for purposes of Article 30. Each of the defined terms is discussed above in the context in which it is used.

Article XV

Article XV of the Protocol deletes and replaces paragraph 1 of Article 32 (Provisions for Implementation) of the Convention. The change revises paragraph 5 so as to remove obsolete cross-reference to provisions of paragraph 4(i) Article 10 and paragraph 8 of Article 30 of the existing Convention.

Article XVI

Article XVI of the Protocol contains the rules for bringing the Protocol into force and giving effect to its provisions.

Paragraph 1

Paragraph 1 provides generally that the Protocol is subject to ratification in accordance with the applicable procedures in the United States and France. Further, the Contracting States shall notify each other by written notification, through diplomatic channels, when their respective constitutional and statutory requirements for the entry into force of the Protocol have been satisfied. The Protocol shall enter into force on the date of receipt of the later of such notifications.

In the United States, the process leading to ratification and entry into force is as follows: Once a treaty has been signed by authorized representatives of the two Contracting States, the Department of State sends the treaty to the President who formally transmits it to the Senate for its advice and consent to ratification, which requires approval by two-thirds of the Senators present and voting. Prior to this vote, however, it generally has been the practice for the Senate Committee on Foreign Relations to hold hearings on the treaty and make a recommendation regarding its approval to the full Senate. Both Government and private sector witnesses may testify at these hearings. After the Senate gives its advice and consent to ratification of the protocol or treaty, an instrument of ratification is drafted for the President's signature. The President's signature completes the process in the United States.

Paragraph 2

The date on which a Protocol enters into force is not necessarily the date on which its provisions take effect. Paragraph 2, therefore, contains rules that determine when the provisions of the Protocol will have effect.

Under subparagraph 2(a), the Protocol will have effect with respect to taxes withheld at source (principally dividends and royalties) for amounts paid or credited on or after the first day of January of the year in which the Protocol enters into force. For example, if the second of the notifications is received on April 25 of a given year, the withholding rates specified in paragraph 2 and 3 of Article 10 (Dividends) would be applicable to any dividends paid or credited on or after January 1 of that year. This rule allows the benefits of the withholding reductions to be put into effect for the entire year the Protocol enters into force. If a withholding agent withholds at a higher rate than that provided by the Protocol (e.g., for payments made before April 25 in the example above), a beneficial owner of the income that is a resident of France may make a claim for refund pursuant to section 1464 of the Code.

Under subparagraph 2(b), the Protocol will have effect with respect to taxes other than those withheld at source for any taxable period beginning on or after January 1 of the year next following entry into force of the Protocol. With respect to taxes on capital, the Convention will have effect for taxes levied on items of capital owned on or after January 1 next following the entry into force of the Protocol.

Paragraph 3

Paragraph 3 provides an exception to the provisions of paragraph 2, incorporating a specific effective date for purposes of the binding arbitration provisions of paragraphs 5 and 6 of Article 26 (Mutual Agreement Procedure) (Article X of the Protocol). Paragraph 3 provides that Article X of the Protocol is effective for cases (i) that are under consideration by the competent authorities as of the date on which the Protocol enters into force and (ii) cases that come under such consideration after the Protocol enters into force. In addition, paragraph 3 provides that the commencement date for cases that are under consideration by the competent authorities as of the date on which the Protocol enters into force is the date the Protocol enters into force. As a result, cases that are unresolved as of the entry into force of the Protocol will go into binding arbitration on the later of two years after the entry into force of the Protocol unless both competent authorities have previously agreed to a different date, and the earliest date upon which the agreement required by subparagraph d) of paragraph 6 of Article 26 has been received by both competent authorities.